THE RESUME SOLUTION

By David Swanson

How to Write (and Use) a Resume That Gets Results

Many helpful worksheets and samples

Step-by-step details on creating
superior resumes and cover letters

Excellent job search tips too

The Resume Solution: How to Write (and Use) a Resume That Gets Results
1995, **JIST Works, Inc.,** Indianapolis, IN

Cover Design: Brad Luther

99 98 97 96 95   1 2 3 4 5 6 7 8 9

This publication is designed to provide accurate and authoritative information in regard to the subject matter covered. It is sold with the understanding that the publisher is not engaged in rendering legal, accounting or other professional advice. If legal advice or other expert assistance is required, the services of a competent professional person should be sought. **From a declaration of principles jointly adopted by a committee of the American Bar Association and a committee of publishers.**

Send all inquiries to:
JIST Works, Inc.
720 North Park Avenue • Indianapolis, IN 46202-3431
Phone: (317) 264-3720   Fax: (317) 264-3709

Library of Congress Cataloging-in-Publication Data

Swanson, Dave, 1935-
     The resume solution : how to write (and use) a resume that gets
results / by David Swanson. -- 2nd ed.
          p. cm.
     "Many helpful worksheets and samples. Step-by-step details on
creating superior resumes and cover letters. Excellent job search
tips too."
  ISBN 1-56370-180-4 : $12.95
  1. Résumés (Employment)   I. Title.
HF5383.S92 1995
650.14--dc20   94-49398
                                                   CIP

ISBN: 1-56370-180-4

This book is dedicated to
many persons rather than to one person:
(I never could make the really tough decisions)
my family, my friends,
my teachers, and my mentors.

Acknowledgments

I appreciate the invaluable assistance of family, friends, mentors, and colleagues…and the people who have attended my speeches, programs, and workshops throughout the world. Without audiences, all speakers are silent.

Richard Nelson Bolles—author of *What Color Is Your Parachute?*—has been my special mentor, teacher, and friend for almost twenty years. His brilliant work, imbued throughout with compassion, has given empowerment to job hunters everywhere. I treasure my work on his staff—and the times with his family at home and abroad.

Wayne Gartley, former Executive Director of the University and College Placement Association of Canada, brought life to the first drafts of this book. Wayne is a longtime friend, and those who know him would agree: he is highly creative, wonderfully witty, and a gifted writer.

Thanks, too, to my friends at JIST Works, Inc.—especially Mike Farr, Sara Hall, Tom Draper, Dr. David Noble, Debi Borst, et al. JIST has become the most successful company of its kind in the world because they truly know the meaning of doing good work.

Scott, Ralph, Ron of Poland, Carol & Dick & Serena, Mike, Betsy, Letta, Jayne, Deb, and others—all know how much they mean to me and to the work we do at Career Seminars.

May you, too, be blessed with friends such as these.

> Today's word
> is forever—
>
> Dave Swanson

Foreword

Resumes are required. Even if you don't like them, they are required. There are times when you really should have one. They are important in the job-hunting and business scene.

But the scene has changed.

Resumes are no longer as important as they were, say the people who receive them.

Decades ago, the mail carrier brought mostly personal letters. Resumes were among the personal things received.

Now, the mail carrier usually brings catalogs...third-class pieces of paper.

Today's resume is not as welcome. It comes with catalogs, with the "junk."

We must create these as very special examples of communication, pieces of paper that will get us in, not keep us out. Resumes are a combination of CALLING CARD, MESSENGER, and VISITOR. They are, indeed, very personal.

For twenty years, I have studied the various factors that make resumes GOOD and BAD.

I have personally read and rated more than twenty thousand resumes! (Most of these rated a 5 or below; a 10 is required!)

The Success Factors are relatively simple. But I have never seen all of them in book form before. And if they were written somewhere, the authors often minced words or gave you so many options that you never figured out which ideas were best.

You have in your hands a book that will put these secrets, this amazing system, within your reach...and with very little effort.

You may react negatively to some of the things I tell you. That is your privilege.

But it is a resume reader's privilege to make judgments about you after reading it. Therefore, it makes only good sense to appear to be "the very best."

This book will do the trick for you.

Read.

Heed.

Succeed.

Table of Contents at a Glance

Chapter 1 *The Resume Basics* 11

Provides examples of different types of resumes; then explains which kind is best for you. Includes job search and networking tips.

Chapter 2 *Collecting Your Thoughts* 23

Teaches you to create effective opening sections of your resume—identification, job objective, and education—through interactive exercises. Helps you secure that "all important" favorable first impression.

Chapter 3 *Tell 'Em What Sells 'Em* 35

Demonstrates, through exercises and examples, how to "sell" yourself in a resume. Explains how to highlight your most impressive accomplishments. Includes helpful advice on getting good references.

Chapter 4 *Designing an Outstanding Resume* 55

Shows you how to design a resume that employers want to read. Emphasizes editing. Gives tips for creating an eye-catching resume.

Chapter 5 *Packaging & Delivering Your Resume* 65

Explains how to make your resume rise above all others. Stresses the importance of readable typefaces, first-class printing, paper color and texture, and more.

Chapter 6 *Sample Resumes & Worksheets* 75

Presents various sample resumes to provide ideas for your own resumes. Features an extensive resume worksheet. Checklist helps you avoid common resume mistakes.

Chapter 7 *The Cover Letter* 163

Emphasizes the importance of the cover letter and shows how to write one for maximum results. Includes sample cover letters.

Chapter 8 *Saying Thank-You & Following Up* 177

Reveals how thank-you notes benefit you during the interview process. Furnishes tips on writing effective thank-you notes, as well as actual samples. Concluding section stresses the importance of following up after every phase of the job search.

Chapter 9 *Job Search Tips* 189

Reviews traditional job search avenues and how to approach them: private and state employment services, personnel offices, and applications. Teaches you how to network to achieve success. Extensive section guides you on how to negotiate salary profitably.

Chapter 10 *Electronic Job Banks* 205

Presents an overview of job searching in the '90s. Reveals advantages and disadvantages of electronic resumes and job banks. Includes examples of electronic resumes.

Chapter 11 *The New Job Market for the Last Half of the '90s* 215

Predicts future trends for what you can expect in the 21st century. Enlightens you about what's needed to get ahead in the new job market.

Epilogue *Is This the End?* 219

Instructs you to adopt "A Philosophy of Job Hunting." Suggests that you take a proactive approach to the job search.

Appendix *Dave Swanson's QUICK GUIDE to Using Resumes* 223

Presents 10 tips for using resumes and cover letters to your best advantage. Shows you an effective way to respond to blind ads.

Table of Contents

▶ **Introduction** I

"Up to the Minute" News about the New Job Market 1
The New Job Market 2
Readable Format Resumes 5
A Few Words on Looking for a Job 6
What This Book Is About 6
The Odds Are Against Most Job Hunters 6
So What's the Secret? 7
My Style Is Your Style 8
So How Do I Make My Resume Stand Out? 8
Speed Reading Your Resume 9

▶ **Chapter I: The Resume Basics** II

Start Your Job Search Right! 11
Some More Words on Looking for a Job 12
So What Are You to Do? 12
Some Job Search Tips 12
    Someone You Know, and Who Likes You,
    Will Hire You 12
    You Can Get to Know Almost Anyone 13
    You Can Get to Know People Who Work in
    Large Organizations 13
    Always Be Honest 13
"This Will Look Good on My Resume" 13
Resume Types 14

Chronological Resumes 14
Functional (or "Skills") Resumes 14
Sample Chronological Resume 14
Sample Functional Resume 16
Which Resume Type Is Right for You? 18
Pros and Cons of a Functional Resume 18
The Combination Resume 19
Sample Combination Resume 19
The Basics of a Good Resume 21

▶ Chapter 2: Collecting Your Thoughts 23

Collect, Organize, and Categorize 23
The First Section, Identification 24
How to Present Your Name 24
Keeping It Simple 24
Using a Middle Name or Initial 25
Presenting Your Address 25
Think about How Your Address Sounds 25
Use a ZIP Code 26
Giving Your Telephone Number 26
Giving an Alternative Number 26
Making a Good Impression 26
Writing Your Address and Phone Number(s) . . . 27
Job Objective 27
Don't Be Vague 27
Make Headlines 28
Education 29
Playing the Grade Game 30
Winning the Grade Game 31
Listing Your Educational Experience 31
Most Recent Educational Experience 32
School Information 33

▶ Chapter 3: Tell 'Em What Sells 'Em 35

Why Are They Looking to Hire You—or Anyone? 35
What Are Accomplishments? 36
What about Results? 36
The RAQ System (Pronounced "Rack") 37
Analyze Your Work Experience 38
The Basics: Selling Your Work Experience 38
Use Action Words 39
Work Experience Worksheets 41
After You Have Documented Your Work Experience 42
Personal Accomplishments 42
Choose Your Most Impressive Results 44
Think Again 45
What Others Say 45
Special Skills 46
Personal Information 46

References 48
    An Added List of References 49
    Letters of Reference 50
    Overcoming Bad References 51
    Using Testimonials in Your Resume 52

▶ Chapter 4: Designing an Outstanding Resume 55

Tailor Your Resume for Excellence 55
The Eye-Strain Approach 56
Edit, Edit, Edit 56
How Long Should Your Resume Be? 57
Secrets of Readability 57
How Do You Read, Learn, and Enjoy? 58
    How the Eye Reads Down a Page 58
    How the Eye Travels Across Lines on a Page 59
    How the Eye Reads Down a Column 59
Use Columns for Eye Appeal 60
Be Your Own Art Director 62

▶ Chapter 5: Packaging & Delivering Your Resume 65

Get Your Resume Noticed 65
Reproducing Your Resume 66
    Typefaces 66
    Sample Typefaces 67
Make Your Resume First Class 68
    Computer-Generated and Typeset Resumes 69
    Acceptable Means of Reproducing Your Resume . . . 69
    Nonacceptable Methods of Reproducing Your Resume 69
    "Maybe" Acceptable Methods of Reproducing Your Resume 70
Evaluating Your Print Shop 70
Selecting the Paper Stock for Your Resume 70
    Color 70
    Texture and Weight 71
Final Touches 72
Stationery and Envelopes 72

▶ Chapter 6: Sample Resumes & Worksheets 75

Choose a Style That Fits 75
    Sample Resumes 76
    Resume Worksheet 155
    References 161
    Common Resume Mistakes Checklist 161
    Test for Readability 162
You're on Your Way 162

►Chapter 7: The Cover Letter

►**Chapter 7: The Cover Letter** 163

The Cover Letter Is Your Introduction 163
Don't Send Cover Letters to Strangers 164
    The Golden Rule for Job Hunters 164
    The Network Advantage 166
Tips on Writing a Good Cover Letter 166
    Write to a Person, Not to a Title 166
    Use a Strong Opening Statement 166
    Keep Your Letter Short, Make It Look Good,
    and Include Key Strengths 167
    Signing Your Cover Letter 168
Sample Cover Letters 168
Broadcast Letters 174
Responding to Want Ads 175

►**Chapter 8: Saying Thank-You & Following Up** 177

The Impact of Good Manners and Thank-You Notes . . . 177
Thanking People in Your Life 178
    Sequence of a Typical Job-Hunting Situation 178
    Send Thank-You Notes or Cards 179
    Choosing Notes, Cards, or Stationery—Size, Style,
    and Color 179
    Do I Write or Print or Type? 179
Some Tips on Writing Good Thank-You Notes 180
Some Sample Thank-You Notes 181
Follow Up! 185
    Following Up before an Interview 185
    Following Up after an Interview 185
    Following Up after Being Rejected 185
    Following Up with Your Network 186
    Following Up and Staying in Control 187
    Following Up by Creating the Environment 187
Keep Smiling 188

►**Chapter 9: Job Search Tips** 189

Additional Tips for Your Job Search 189
Private Employment Services 189
State Employment Services 190
Personnel Offices 190
Applications 192
    Be Prepared 192
    Filling Out Applications 193
    The Last Word on Filling Out Applications 194
The Road Less Traveled: A More Effective Way 194
Networking—When It Works and When It Doesn't 195
    First: Friends and Relatives 195
    Develop New "Acquaintances" 196
    Get Referrals to Supervisors and Managers, Too . . . 196
Ask for an Interview Even If There Are No Openings . . 197

    Keep Following Up 197
        Send Resumes 197
        Call! 198
        Send Notes 198
    Use the *Yellow Pages* 198
    Walk In, Anyway 199
    Some Tips for Negotiating Salary 199
        Salaries and Earnings in Your Chosen Field 200
        How Does This Organization Pay Its People? 201
        Salary Information in Other Organizations 201
    How to Answer "The Big Question" 201
    What Comes Next? 203
    A Final Word on Money 203

▶**Chapter 10: Electronic Job Banks** 205
    A Few Words on "The Latest Way to Job Hunt" 205
    The Primary Advantage of Electronic Resumes
    and Job Banks 209
    What Electronic Resumes Look Like 211
    How Important Are the New Electronic Techniques? . . 214

▶**Chapter 11: The New Job Market for
the Last Half of the '90s** 215
    What to Expect in the 21st Century 215
    What's Needed to Get Ahead 216

▶**Epilogue: Is This the End?** 219
    Having a Purpose 219
    Adopting "A Philosophy of Job Hunting" 220
    Empowering Yourself 220
    Acting 220
    Living 221

▶**Appendix: Dave Swanson's QUICK GUIDE
to Using Resumes** 223

Introduction

"Up to the Minute" News about the New Job Market

The "New Job Market" has arrived! It's here—we think!—for the rest of the 1990s. And compared to the job market we knew, we don't recognize the new "thing." The job market has really *reinvented* itself—and it has *almost completely* transformed its inner structure. The insides of the 1980s Job Market, and the Market that existed during the years before that, simply look *different* from this New Job Market.

The structure and the inner workings have changed dramatically, but—SURPRISE!—**the outside *appears* to look about the same.**

And it fools us—by allowing us to think that because it "looks the same," it's the same as it was.

That's why job hunters, including people laid off by the tens and hundreds of thousands, who haven't realized what the changes are—and how revolutionary they are—are being caught in a bad situation. They're using old tools for new tasks.

It's as though you were going on a vacation from your home in Ohio to Aunt Minnie's in California...and you had a full week for yourself to enjoy your vacation...and then, you went out to your driveway, climbed into your car, and drove West.

What would happen?

Well, concerning a vacation, almost nothing. You'd either get halfway to California and realize your mistake...or you would arrive there and then discover you had to turn around and come back because you'd not planned correctly and had no time to spend visiting your aunt and relaxing.

Results you achieved: none!

Effort you expended: quite a bit.

Money you spent: too much—on gas, motels, meals, etc.

What was wrong?

You failed to analyze what the problem was, and you failed to use the best means to solve it.

(You should have flown!)

So, instead of looking for a vacation, let's suppose you're looking for a new job. A career.

Something you've trained for. Gone to school for. Borrowed money to make possible.

This time, though, you want a *good* job.

No more of these jobs where you work long hours—and no more jobs where you're doing things most of the time that *you don't even like doing.*

So you go looking.

You do what you've been told, of course: you look in the papers—"to see what's out there."

Hmmm. Not much there this week. Maybe next week will be better. Or maybe you should try the out-of-town papers—from the "fast-growth parts of the country."

Not much next week, either. Hmmmm.

You're listed with the college careers office. But it doesn't seem to have anything for 35-year-old alums.

And you decide to go looking and list yourself with the local Job Service office—just in case it has something. People tell you it never does, but—just in case—you go.

Hmmmm. Nothing is turning up there, either.

The economy is supposed to be getting better, isn't it? The recession is over, right? And especially here, where *you* live. The recession wasn't even that bad here, was it?

No, it wasn't. But that's not the problem. What's wrong, is this: you are doing things just the way your grandfather did, and the way your father and mother did (and it never even worked that well for them, did it?). (Or *are* you the grandchild of a Rockefeller or J. Paul Getty?)

So your lesson is this: **OLD TRICKS DON'T WORK WELL, IF AT ALL, IN THE NEW JOB MARKET!**

So let's tell you **what's new**—and then tell you how to attack this **New** Beast—and come out the Winner!

▶ The New Job Market

The job market for this decade has brought the following profound changes.

1. Layoffs from large corporations have continued at a record pace, resulting in huge numbers of highly skilled and qualified people, at all levels, competing for jobs against one another. *This will continue.* "You ain't seen nothin' yet!" Thus far, it has been a fact of life

in the largest companies; when it hits the almost-large, the medium, and other smaller firms, you'll see even more dramatic changes. Will it? Of course. It will hit almost everyone eventually.

2. Your *protections*—for employees and workers against losing their jobs—have become as rare as the dodo bird. It doesn't seem to matter whether you are an ace-professional, superqualified and making $150,000, or a struggling young college grad with a family to support, trying to get by on $25,000. Security in the workplace is almost nonexistent.

3. Labor unions, for decades the protectors of the "little person," are having their own troubles—which include even staying alive. In the past 20 years, membership in unions (organizations that you thought would go to bat for you when things got tough—and to which you paid millions of dollars for that service) has declined from 35 percent of the work force in 1960 to just 11 percent! Their operating budgets are down, and their power is crippled; and although some improvement has been seen in union membership rolls, the overall trend is expected to continue **downward.**

4. The kinds of jobs once "reserved" and available only "for males" (men were the acknowledged breadwinners for families back then) have disappeared *faster* than expected! Instead of large factories breaking up into smaller factories, which we thought would then employ the workers (perhaps at lower wages and salaries, and with fewer benefits, but nonetheless *employ* them), the number of new factory jobs created has been dismally small.

   The work once done by "real men," such as your grandfathers, is now done by automated, electronically controlled, computer-directed, ultra-high-tech machines and robots.

   And if not done by machines that replace high-cost people who require high-cost benefits, those jobs are sent to another state, or another country, where we can pay less in labor costs and fringe benefits so that we can stay in business as an organization, rather than have our companies go bankrupt because we can't compete on costs. *Men who did this kind of work are having the most profound difficulties coping in this New Job Market.*

5. Job opportunities for females, however, are booming. Not only are the white-collar office, computer, administrative, and other jobs once reserved almost exclusively for females increasing at a spectacularly high rate (while the "men's jobs" mentioned above go *down-down-down*), but the jobs once thought of as "men's work" are now for females too. Gender equity has definitely arrived, although you won't hear many people acknowledge it.

   Is this good news? You bet it is! The more *good* people we have competing for jobs, the better the quality of the person who is selected to do the work. Male or female, young or old, the *best-qualified people* are no longer a pie-in-the-sky wish; if you don't find and hire the best people, someone else will—and your own products and services will be below the level of acceptability.

In the male-dominated past, we were effectively depriving ourselves of 50 percent of our potential brainpower. Gender equity, as it integrates itself fully, will help us lead the way as a nation.

6. Normal sources for recruiting employees have become as dry as desert oases. Employees *of the type that high-tech and new-age organizations need* are harder and harder to find. And if employers *do* manage to locate qualified candidates, the odds are that those candidates don't want to work as hard as they must when they're on the job. If companies use "normal sources," they get either *too many applicants* or *too few applicants,* or they get *"no one who's qualified."* Because companies need fewer people than in the 1960s and 1970s, recruiting budgets have been slashed.

    One Fortune 500 company, which formerly recruited a few thousand engineers annually nationwide, has cut its annual college recruiting budget by 85 percent and its hiring objectives by 90 percent.

7. People work more and longer hours now, not less; we work harder, stay there longer each day, play less—and our "real" pay is less than it was 10 years ago (now that a $14,000 car has risen to $24,000, a luxury car costs $30,000 or more, and a box of cereal is $4.50).

8. We have failed to come to grips, as individual human beings faced with thousands of career options and choices, with the ultimate question: "What do you want to do?"

    People answer this just about as they did 40 years ago: undecided and unfocused. Students get very little guidance, even at the so-called best schools—the high schools, the prep schools, the colleges, the universities, and (yes) even the graduate schools. Adults reply to "What are you looking for?" by either relating "What I've done before" or stabbing in the dark at something they think might be better. Has this improved since 1980?

    WHAT DO YOU THINK?

    Of course it hasn't.

9. Failures and mistakes are now *encouraged* by the top management consultants and gurus: "If you don't allow your people to experiment, to be creative, to use their brains, your organization will not be a leader and an innovator...and you'll be out of business!" That's good advice—**great** advice!

    But people hunting for jobs *can't make these mistakes* when they're making career decisions and marketing themselves! This is *not* the time to "try things out"—unless you're independently wealthy and can afford to take a few years off and experiment to your heart's content. (The time to try things out is while you're gainfully employed, but on your own time, to experiment and see where you want to make your next move, and how you will make it!)

    Job-hunting is not a shopping expedition! It is a very focused, almost-scientific process. But in addition, it requires a great deal of creativity. (See our new section on KNOWLEDGE, and you'll see what we mean—and what to do.)

Have job hunters progressed in this new age? Are *they* doing better? Have they *caught on* that "old methods don't work" in the new age of employment? WHAT DO YOU THINK?

Of course they haven't!

▶ Readable Format Resumes

Have resumes changed in the last five years? No.

Are they better now? No.

Are they more creative? A little.

Is that good? No.

The most expensive resume book we've seen—and we've seen almost all of them—is a *beauty!* But it's not very *good.*

If you want to buy a book to show off beautiful resumes to your friends, please write me; I'll gladly tell you the name of this book and the publisher.

If you want to know how to create and use a resume that will *do the job* for you, you've already bought the right book. It's not the most expensive, but the information is *the right stuff,* and you'll not find it anywhere else—as far as we know.

Here's where they go wrong:

Mistake #1. They use the wrong typeface—usually a sans-serif one—so the resume becomes 75 percent **less** readable.

Mistake #2. They use the wrong layout; they write across-the-page, instead of in a narrower column, so that the resume becomes **less** readable.

Mistake #3. They use even or straight margins on both the right and left sides (instead of a ragged or uneven margin on the right side, which is much better). The result is that the computer gains control of your all-important spacing, and the resume becomes **less** readable.

Mistake #4. They crowd everything into one or two pages because someone told you that "no one will read it if it's longer than one or two pages."

NONSENSE!

The corrected statement is this: "No one will read it—if it is not **readable.**"

A crowded resume *is* **much less** readable.

Mistake #5. They spend hundreds of dollars on hiring a professional to write your resume for you, instead of encouraging you to take the time and the care to prepare 90 percent of your resume yourself. If you prefer, when you have completed 90 percent of the work, you can go to the professional, for much less money, to have her or him put a finishing touch on it, or to make suggestions, or to print it.

But don't let "the professional" do **anything** to make your resume **less readable!**

ASIDE: *THIS IS IMPORTANT*—so take two minutes and read it carefully:

You'd be surprised how many people have come to our offices, workshops, or seminars for resume critiques—people who have paid $100, $250, or more for a resume and who are *astonished* when we show them one of our **readable format resumes** for comparison.

Our comparison test is simple: we simply ask a person to think of herself as a corporate executive who has been assigned to screen candidates' resumes. "You have 500 resumes to screen; your job is to find (no more than) 10 people who best meet our needs, so that we can consider these 10 more seriously. Now, take a look at these two."

We have **their** expensive, normally designed resume hanging down from one hand—and one of our inexpensive-or-free **readable format resumes** hanging down from the other hand.

We let her glance at each one, just as she would if she were screening hundreds at an office, for about five seconds. Then we ask, "Which one of these two will you more likely set aside to actually read...and spend some time with? Which one looks better to you?"

The results and answers **never** vary: **Every time,** he or she chooses the **readable format resume.**

►A Few Words on Looking for a Job

"Prepare the camel's hump in the usual way . . ."
So began a recipe I once saw in a gourmet cookbook.
Many job hunting books...and experts...and job counselors...offer the same sort of bewildering instructions: "Prepare your resume and take or mail it to employers."
It all sounds so easy!
Or does it?

►What This Book Is About

This book is about writing a *superior* resume.
A resume that will stand out in a crowd. A resume that will be read.
This is also a book about getting a job. I assume that this is your reason for wanting a resume to begin with.

►The Odds Are Against Most Job Hunters

No matter how good your resume is (and most of them are *not* good at all), the odds are against most job hunters from the start.
Why?
Because they don't know how to write a good resume. They don't know how to use their resume. And they don't know how the job market works.

Job hunters don't realize that employers may receive *hundreds,* or even *thousands,* of resumes every single week (whether the employers advertise for applicants in the newspaper or not) and that it is very easy for resumes to be lost in the shuffle.

This is especially true of large, well-known companies:

- Airlines
- Manufacturers of "brand name"products
- Broadcasting companies
- Advertising agencies

As an example, one airline, which hired some 300 flight attendants in one year, received over *750,000* letters, applications, and resumes for 300 positions. The astounding fact about all these resumes sent by job hunters every day is that the majority of the resumes are incredibly poorly prepared.

They get only a fleeting glance from overworked, harried personnel directors before the resumes are tossed onto the rejection pile.

What are the chances that the writer of a poorly prepared or illegible resume will be selected for an interview? *Practically none!*

Scarce company resources make it impossible to interview every job applicant. (In most companies, it would take an army of interviewers working around the clock if all the people who applied for jobs were interviewed.)

And many, if not most, resumes are from job applicants who are *not* qualified for the jobs for which they are applying.

These resumes get what they deserve: rejection. The people employed to screen resumes must weed out the unlikely job applicants; only the most promising people are selected for interviews.

The ratio of resumes to people selected may be 10-to-one, 100-to-one, or 1000-to-one in any particular company. But you can be sure that few of those who submit a resume will be called for a personal interview.

►So What's the Secret?

There's no magic formula for getting a good job. Even the "perfect" resume can't do that for you. But I can help you increase your chances of getting that job by producing a superior resume.

And teaching you how to use it.

Like dieting, writing the best possible resume will take some hard work on your part. But the results will be well worth the effort.

I've read just about all the career planning/job hunting books that have flooded the bookstores in the past few years, but none of these has offered the inside information on the particular techniques of resume writing I will reveal in this book.

I do not intend to duplicate the excellent career planning/job hunting system forged by my mentor, Richard Nelson Bolles, in the best-selling *What Color Is Your Parachute?* Better you should buy a copy and read it immediately if you haven't already done so...and act on the advice contained in this revolutionary book.

No, I am going to assume that you already have a good idea of what skills you have and want to use in a job...and have defined some ideal jobs.

I'm going to show you how to develop a superior, readable resume. A resume that will produce the results you want.

And get you the job you want! The job that is right for you!

▶ My Style Is Your Style

I'll give you tips that are guaranteed to make your resume superior-looking, superior-reading, and will ensure that it gets *read*.

But the greatest gift I have for you is information on how to *do your own resume,* using powerful secrets and proven techniques. To do otherwise, to copy the standard "Harvard Graduate School of Business Resume Forms" or turn over this chore to a "professional" resume-writing service, would be a *mistake.*

Why? Because no one knows *you* as *you* do! And because—if you go to one of the resume mills or career counseling outfits that also provides resume services—you may be putting yourself in line for a slap.

Executives and personnel people aren't stupid. One "career counseling" firm (now thankfully forced out of business by a series of news articles and the government itself) provided a "model" resume to each of its clients at "no extra charge."

So, for $2,500, they would package you into *their* recommended format. When personnel directors saw these resumes arrive—often several at a time—always printed on the same color paper in the same slightly unusual size, they knew what they had: people who weren't sharp enough to do a resume by themselves.

Those resumes, needless to say, found their way into the famed "circular file" by the fastest possible method. They weren't even paid the courtesy of a form-letter reply.

So, if you want it done right (with results from your resume), do it yourself!

▶ So How Do I Make My Resume Stand Out?

A resume is like an advertisement...a sales brochure of your special skills and training that will appeal to potential employers.

Of course, you are not qualified for every job that exists in today's complex employment market any more than one manufacturer's product is suited for every consumer's needs.

Neither would you want to work for every employer, nor in every job available. So you must do what any company with a product or service to sell does.

- Prepare your message so that it will be read and considered by your target audience—in this case, those who can hire you in a job of your choice.

- Evaluate your abilities accurately.

- Research your market fully.

Companies spend billions of dollars annually to produce advertisements that will appeal to readers of magazines and newspapers. They want you to *read* their message and *act on it.*

Something in your resume must *click,* must grab the reader's attention, for it to be considered over all the others.

▶Speed Reading Your Resume

No one will spend much time reading your resume in detail. In fact, thirty seconds is a long time for the average screener to spend on a resume.

More Likely, your resume will receive only 10 to 15 seconds of their time —unless you capture their attention immediately in the initial glance at it.

You must prepare your resume, using the same techniques advertisers use to give you an edge over your competition.

So that your resume will be *read!*

- Not ignored.
- Not passed over.
- Not rejected.
- But *read!*
- And *considered.*

You will learn how to design and test your resume for layout and readability. And to consider your resume's impact on potential employers.

And you will learn how to use a resume effectively in your job search. Which is what a resume is all about.

Or should be.

Chapter 1
The Resume Basics

Start Your Job Search Right!

Some frustrated people have used their resumes for wallpaper. But, more likely, you want to use yours for finding a *job*. Which seems reasonable enough. But you do need to realize a few facts:

- At its best, your resume may help you get an interview.

- If you use your resume in the traditional way—sending it to someone you don't know in a large organization—your resume is more likely to be ignored than read.

Before I begin to show you how to create a superior resume, it is essential that you understand how resumes are *best* used.

And why this is so.

▶Some More Words on Looking for a Job

Most job seekers believe they need to send out many resumes to personnel departments to get a job. And some do get jobs in just this way. But times are changing! About 75 percent of all business organizations don't even have personnel offices. They are small organizations, where over *seventy percent of all new jobs are being created.*

So if you insist on sending out resumes to personnel departments, you are missing most of the available jobs. And much of the opportunity.

Even organizations which *do* have personnel departments are far more likely to "file" your resume than do anything helpful with it. They get entirely too many resumes to do otherwise. So they will give yours a quick look over and then they will put it away, in all probability, with the others, there to rest for eternity. Or until someone throws it away.

In the unlikely event that your resume just happens to come in when an appropriate job opens up—for someone with just your experience and training—you might get an interview. But probably not, because it is most likely that your resume was set aside, in the reject pile. Rejected, even though you could do the job. Because your resume was dull. Or because it was too long. Or whatever the case.

The person who looked it over, along with 25 (or 200) other resumes in the pile, had no idea of the dedicated person you are. They just had your resume. And it didn't catch their attention.

▶So What Are You to Do?

You, because you have read this book (and have done all the activities), will have a superior resume. Your resume will stand out from all the others. And get you the attention you deserve. But you should also understand that most hiring is not done by a stranger hiring an applicant who is unknown to her or him. Hiring is generally done by people who already know an applicant. So your next employer will probably be someone you know. And one of the reasons you'll be hired is that they will know you and *trust* you. They will also believe that you can do the job and that you will do it reliably and well.

No resume can do this whole "getting hired" process for you. Not even the one I will show you how to create. Only "you" can do the real work of getting hired.

▶Some Job Search Tips

I will give you more job search tips throughout this book, particularly in the last chapter.

But there are several important points for you to remember.

Someone You Know, and Who Likes You, Will Hire You

- You probably don't know them yet, nor do they know you. But you will meet during your search for a job. And you will like each other enough to work together.

- Which brings up an important fact that you should not ignore: most people get their jobs—as many as 40 percent of them—from leads provided by friends, relatives, or acquaintances. Not from someone they don't know. So your task is to avoid, as much as possible, depending on strangers. Resumes sent to "Dear Mr./Ms. Personnel Department" will be treated just the way you treat the "Dear Occupant" mail you get. Like junk mail, they will be discarded, with few exceptions.

You Can Get to Know Almost Anyone

- I was once told that you can get to almost anyone, even the President, through just three to six levels of personal contacts. Just ask someone you know for the name of someone who knows someone who knows the President. And so it is in the job search. The process is called *networking*. For example, ask each of your friends and relatives for the name of someone who might know about a job opening that requires a person with your skills. You will come to know more people than you could ever imagine. If you ask this same question of each person you are referred to, you will meet more people than you can count. And one of them will hire you!

You Can Get to Know People Who Work in Large Organizations

- It's not difficult to get the name of the person in any organization who is most likely to hire someone like you. You can ask your friends and relatives if they know anyone who works there—or if they know someone else who might know. Or you can use the *Yellow Pages* to call the organization. And ask them, "Who is in charge of such and such?" In most cases, you can get right to them. Ask if you can come in to see them about any future job openings, even if none are open just now. *Then* send them your resume. And a thank you note for their precious time. Even if they can't see you now.

- It takes only a minute or so to make these personal contacts. And they can make *all* the difference.

Always Be Honest

- Your resume does not need to mention that you eat crackers in bed. We all have things we don't tell strangers. But it is dishonest to say you can handle something you cannot or that you have done something you have not done. Too many job seekers think they have to overstate what they can do to get hired. And as a result, too many resumes are not believable.

- Most employers will see right through an inflated resume. They won't hire a dishonest person. Nor would you. But some people do convince employers to hire them for jobs they can't do well. And, too often, they then lose the jobs. Or, even worse, they come to hate their jobs. And themselves. So, while this book is about creating delightfully *readable* resumes, it is also about getting a job. A job you can grow in. And enjoy.

▶"This Will Look Good on My Resume"

It's amazing how many people have used this reason for taking a certain job or training. We've all said it (and we've heard others say it) over and over again. It's as if we feel that everything we do in our work life must make our resume look good. But your resume should present a mirror image of your life (seen in the best possible light) rather than vice versa. And I'm now going to take you, step-by-step, through the construction of a superior-looking resume—a resume that will work wonders for you in your job hunt.

A resume that will be *read.*

►Resume Types

Before you begin writing your resume, you should be aware of the different types of resumes. There are at least seven different types of resumes:

- Chronological
- Functional (also called a skills resume)
- Combination (combines chronological and functional)
- Narrative
- Teaching
- Curriculum vitae
- Creative

If all this seems confusing, remember: if it looks like a duck, walks like a duck, and quacks like a duck, it's a duck! A resume is a resume is a resume—no matter how you design it or what name you give it. The chief distinction between types of resumes is whether they are *chronological* or *functional.*

Chronological Resumes

A *chronological* resume stresses time—*when* you went to school or had a certain job. Thus you state in your resume that from September 1993 to May 1994 you worked at Foster Steel Foundries or you attended Bloom College. Every year, every month, and almost every day of your working life is accounted for in such a resume.

Functional (or "Skills") Resumes

A *functional* resume stresses your skills and is organized by skills, duties, or functions, as shown in the example that follows later in this chapter.

Sample Chronological Resume

The resume on the following page illustrates a typical chronological resume which lists organizations where you have worked. They are listed in *reverse* order, beginning with your present, or most recent, employer. Your *first* full-time job is listed last and is usually given less space. You should give less-detailed descriptions of accomplishments, duties, and responsibilities of your earliest jobs.

Chronological resumes are the most commonly used type. Because employers are used to seeing them, they find chronological resumes easy to read and follow.

Barbara A. McGinty
7236 Buena Vista Circle
Milwaukee, Wisconsin 53202
(414) 555-4465
(414) 444-4661 (messages)

CAREER OBJECTIVE:
Customer Service Supervisor/Manager

WORK EXPERIENCE

1991 to 1994

Guard Insurance Company
Milwaukee, Wisconsin

Customer Service Administrator

- Provided customer and general agent information in Pro Division. Processed policy changes, agent commissions, bill adjustments and corrections, audits, and accounts receivable in excess of $30 million. Utilized CRT system daily. Received "Service Management Award."

1989 to 1991

Telephone Information Systems
Milwaukee, Wisconsin

Customer Service Representative

- Authorized new account credit approvals, monitored collections, followed up on slow-pays, provided information for customer billing and equipment. Sold additional telephone services.

1988 to 1989

Wrap 'n' Ship
Milwaukee, Wisconsin

Store Manager

- Managed retail store providing UPS, wrapping, packaging, shipping, and other services. Supervised three employees. Resolved customer problems. Maintained all permanent records for business.

1987 to 1988

Real Estate Sales Agent

- Independently listed, presented, and sold real estate properties.

EDUCATION

- Brandon College, Milwaukee
  Completed 31 credits in business courses

- University of Wisconsin-Milwaukee
  Completed additional courses for degree in Public Relations and Mass Communications

Sample Functional Resume

The typical functional resume lists the kinds of functions you performed on the jobs you have held. The functions are grouped together by their relationship to one another or by projects or assignments. This resume emphasizes the *skills* you have, rather than the places you have worked or the periods of time you worked at each organization. *Functional* resumes are used less often than *chronological* resumes.

There are pros and cons for each type.

Barbara H. Martinson
9612 W. Capstan Road
Sea View, California 92134
(714) 555-1537
Message: (714) 555-1657

JOB TARGET: Computer Programmer, using COBOL, C, or
                               similar languages

SCHOOL ACHIEVEMENTS:

- **Honor Student,** Mount Diablo City College, Sea View, California.
  Graduate with Associate Degree in computer technology, May, 1990.
  3.42 grade average.

- **Student Leader** in various campus organizations; President, Office
  Education Association; member, Student Council (2 years); chairper-
  son, Campus Ride Pool.

- **High School Honor Student.** Active in various sports, clubs, musical
  organizations.

WORK EXPERIENCE

- **Organized and ran office** for local insurance office (four agents);
  Developed new filing system. Operated IBM PC with terminal access
  to IBM mainframe. Developed and implemented new claims reminder
  procedures for agents. Improved typing from 55 wpm to 75 wpm.

- **Raised $4,000 for charity** through Office Education Association fund
  drive, pizza sales; proceeds went to Special Olympics.

- **Selected as Laboratory Assistant** in Data Processing Lab at school.
  Used background knowledge to advise insurance agency on new hardware and software purchases for office.

PERSONAL

- Earned funds to pay own school expenses. Worked at insurance office
  (above) and at supermarket while in high school. Hardworking, willing
  to relocate.

Which Resume Type Is Right for You?

If you have an excellent work record and educational background and you can account for each segment of your life, the chronological resume may be fine for you. But if you have any gaps that you don't want to include in your resume (like the year you were unemployed because you just didn't feel like working...or backpacked around Europe...or whatever), including dates will immediately raise the question, "What was she doing during this time?" Employers are suspicious of gaps in a resume. When they spot or detect a gap, or a period of months or years you don't explain, they assume the worst. If your resume omits the months and years in which you worked at each place, you'll be "suspect."

Remember—the traditional selection process is a negative one. Employers use resumes to screen people out. They toss out many resumes before they choose the small number of people they will consider hiring. You might use a functional resume if the dates when you acquired your skills or worked in a particular job have little to do with the job you're applying for now.

Absolutely right! But you're making a major mistake in your viewpoint. Always try to see things from the reader's point of view, rather than from your own. People who read large numbers of resumes are, from experience, suspicious.

In a functional resume, you usually list your most marketable or highly prized skills first. And your special accomplishments, honors, or awards, regardless of when you acquired them.

Many supporters of functional resumes say the chronological resume makes it too easy for employers to screen you out. They say, correctly, that you'll be rejected for being too young, too old, having too much experience in one job, for not having moved up rapidly enough, and on and on. And remember that you're trying to *remove* reasons for being screened out. It shouldn't matter that you earned your B.A. in 1975 (or 1965 or whenever) rather than in 1994. Or that you learned to supervise people in 1981 rather than more recently. The question is or should be: Do you now have the skills needed to do this job well?

But before you decide to use a purely functional resume, let's look at the advantages and disadvantages of such a resume so you can see what you're up against.

Pros and Cons of a Functional Resume

A functional resume can do these good things for you:

- Remove emphasis on age
- Place emphasis on results
- Show skills you have and how you have used them
- Be ideal for returning-to-work housewives, mothers, students, and others who haven't done paid-for work for some time
- Lets you transfer skills into results..."old" jobs into skills that are in demand

A functional resume makes these problems for you:

- Its lack of chronology makes your resume *different* because most resumes are chronological.

- Its lack of chronology also may lead to the suspicion you're covering up something bad, even if you're not.
- It is more difficult to follow and read.
- It makes it difficult to find your *most recent* experience, which is what most employers are willing to pay for...and on which they may base salary, level, and so on.
- It can seem devious to some readers.

So put yourself in the *reader's* place and think about what type of resume will work best for you.

The Combination Resume

The *combination* resume combines elements of the chronological and functional resumes. It may be a solution for people who insist on avoiding an out-and-out chronological listing of the months and years they have worked at each job. Such a resume incorporates the best features of functional and chronological resumes. For many people, this is the format I suggest they consider.

Sample Combination Resume

On the next page is a typical combination resume. It combines elements of the chronological resume and the functional or skills resume. The combination resume may be best for certain situations, even though it is slightly more difficult for readers to follow, because sections of the resume do not follow in a perfectly logical order.

Nancy B. Farraday
678 14th Street, Apartment 1B
Louisville, Kentucky 40200
(502) 555-3386 (home)
(502) 555-6244 (answering service)

Job Objective: Manufacturer's Representative, Consumer Products

SALES EXPERIENCE

- Responsible for company's drapery marketing activities in four-state territory (Oklahoma, Kansas, Missouri, and Arkansas). Established brand new territory; made all sales calls and contacts for $20-million manufacturer and distributor of draperies sold to multifamily apartment housing industry.

- Consistently ranked in top 5 of 14-person drapery sales force (eight other territories were established). Sales averaged $75,000 monthly (four states).

- Active in six local clubs and organizations for professional real estate and property management.

- Sold, designed, programmed, and installed new electronic point-of-purchase cash record systems for retail use (stores, restaurants, malls, offices). Opened and successfully managed new territory in northern suburbs of Atlanta.

- Exceeded monthly sales quotas by average of 35% in Atlanta territory. New customers accounted for 75% of sales. Awarded incentive trip to Mexico.

- As District Manager for Florida nad Georgia Region, increased sales for Chicago-based manufacturer of small appliances 71% over prior year. Cited by manager for "outstanding performance and results."

WORK HISTORY

- Hart's Mills Draperies, Atlanta, Georgia, 1988-Present

- Electronix Cash Systems, Atlanta, Georgia, 1984-1988

- General Appliances, Chicago, Illinois, 1982-1984

EDUCATION

- Bachelor of Science degree in Business Administration
  Northern Illinois University, DeKalb, Illinois, 1984
- Graduate Studies, Computing Programming, M.B.A.
  Georgia State University, Atlanta, 1986-1987

▶ The Basics of a Good Resume

No matter what type of resume you decide to use, you'll need a lot of time to do your best resume. One draft won't do it! In fact, it may take four or five drafts to complete a resume you'll be proud to send out. You must edit, edit, edit…down to a manageable length. You need to tailor your resume to what the reader wants to read, instead of saying everything you'd love to say about yourself.

No matter how well qualified you may be, the design and readability of your resume will be most important to the reader. The design—the look and the graphics of your resume—will determine whether your resume will be *read* at all. That's the purpose of this book. There are many resume books on the market. This one is designed to show you how to have the *best* resume possible, based on content, design, and readability.

Finally, I want you to be invited to an interview and to be offered the job you want! This book—and your new resume—will help!

Chapter 2
Collecting Your Thoughts

Collect, Organize, and Categorize

Before you begin considering design and readability—the basis for your successful resume you need to collect the "raw material" of your life. This chapter will help you organize your history into the following useful categories for resume writing:

- Identification
- Career objective
- Areas of effectiveness
- Work experience
- Education

- School activities
- Community activities
- Personal data
- Special Skills
- References

In this chapter and the next, I will guide you in completing each of these sections for use in your resume. This will be basic, unedited material, so don't try to put it in final form yet. Later, it will form the basis for your resume content.

Now, you can begin to begin! Complete each section in pencil (which will allow you to make changes), following the instructions. This is important work, but it is easy. So if you want to complete it while listening to music or watching light TV, you might find the task more enjoyable.

►The First Section, Identification

Do you need the word "RESUME" at the top of the page? Not necessarily. It's probably best to omit it.

Almost anyone you're sending your resume to will immediately recognize what it is. And if they don't..., well, maybe you shouldn't be sending them your resume in the first place.

Of course, you should begin with your name, placed at the top of the page.

How to Present Your Name

Use your most businesslike name. For most people, that will be your full name, with an initial, such as Shirley A. Sweeney or B. Scott Janis.

If you have a "real name" that you neither use nor like, use the one by which you are known. For example, if a man named Buckhampton R. Jones dislikes his first name, he might use any one of the following alternative forms:

Hampton R. Jones *or*
B. Robert (Bob) Jones *or*
Buck R. Jones *or*
Buckhampton R. (B. R.) Jones

If you use a hyphenated last name, such as Marita Ann Schillingworth-Gieselo, consider the possibility that the form of your name may have a negative impact on the reader. Any difficult-to-pronounce combination of words may make the reader think that the resume itself will be difficult to read.

If you ever wrestled with the question "Shall I read this Dostoevsky novel or not?" you probably picked up the heavy book and considered the names themselves in your decision. More than likely, you said, "This is going to be difficult, not something I can read lightly in my leisure time."

Why would the people who read your resume be any different? They're not. They are turned off by difficult words, including names.

So if you do have the option, use a form of your name that makes reading easiest for the reader.

Keeping It Simple

On your resume, then, you might consider using just "one" last name, the one you prefer using for business. Some people find that having a business name (a name that is easy to spell and pronounce) is valuable to them.

(Some friends of mine have complained for years, only half-seriously, about having to spell their names every time they use them, or about having them mispronounced by virtually everyone.)

A businesswoman I know, whose last name is Mule, has the informational phrase "pronounced Mool" beneath her name on her business card. I agree. This is a considerate and kind way to handle a possibly difficult problem for the recipient.

Make your name easy to understand, easy to read, and easy to pronounce. Think of the reader, not of yourself. You can easily clear up any misunderstandings or mispronunciations during your interview.

If your name is unusually complicated—has many middle names, difficult spellings, and so on—simplify it!

Using a Middle Name or Initial

Should you use a middle initial? Maybe. Some people consider it stuffy and pompous. But if you have a very common last name, such as Johnson, Smith or Jones, you may want to distinguish yourself by using your middle name or your middle initial.

Middle names, too, seem a bit too much for resumes, unless you need the extra name to offset the possibility that two people with the same name are applying for the job.

Now, write your name here—in the most acceptable way—to create the best impression for yourself:

(First name)	(Middle initial or name)	(Last name)

Presenting Your Address

Use the best-sounding address you have, without abbreviations (which make reading/skimming more difficult, not less!).

If you have a post office box, consider using your "real" address instead. A house number is usually more impressive and substantial-sounding than a post office box.

Here are some examples:

- Margaret Samuels-Berlinsky
  7755 Colorado Circle
  Dayton, Ohio 45472-8813

- Barton E. Commerly
  Apartment #308
  1455 N. 86th Street
  New York, New York 10744-4346

- John Malchow
  5775 Columbus Street
  Odessa, Texas 72241-1648

- Lucille Weyker
  2254 Ludington Terrace
  San Diego, California 90277-6862

If your address is correctly written:

> 1567 Wilson Terrace (rear cottage)

consider eliminating the (rear cottage) portion. And if you have two addresses —your permanent address and your school address—you may want to use both.

Think about How Your Address Sounds

The name of your city or hometown says something about you, your personality, and the ways in which prospective employers may perceive you. Such judgments and opinions may not be fair, but they do exist.

For example, if you are asked "Where are you from?" when visiting Europe, and you say, "Chicago," the response will likely be "Oh! Gangster! Bang-bang!" If, on the other hand, you say "Northern Illinois, where there are many farms," you will be perceived differently.

If you list Beverly Hills as your address, you'll get a slightly different reaction than if you say Los Angeles.

Therefore, you may accurately say that you live in Milwaukee, Wisconsin, when you actually live in the neighboring village of Sussex, which is "out in the country," and which your reader may not recognize.

The reader will probably know where Milwaukee is, however. And she may also imagine you have a more sophisticated personality if your home address is in a city of 25,000 or 30,000, or 500,000 or more, rather than an unknown suburb.

Use a ZIP Code

A 9-digit ZIP code enables the post office to deliver mail to your home or building, without further identification on an envelope. So if you list your 9-digit ZIP code, you may have a bit of latitude in naming the city in which you live.

Obviously, if you live in a small town, with no city nearby, you will give the name of your town and the correct ZIP code. If you do not know your 9-digit ZIP code, a call to your local postmaster should bring you the answer in a few minutes.

The 9-digit ZIP code is preferred in all business situations.

Giving Your Telephone Number

Give the area code and number where you may be reached most of the time.

If you are difficult to reach, you should have an answering machine. Use a businesslike message, not a Bette Davis voice or Jack Benny comedy skit! Then the prospective employer can leave a message without having to call back a dozen times in futile efforts to reach you.

If you're hard to reach by phone, the employer may well decide to give up after an attempt or two, just as you would do.

Giving an Alternative Number

If you like, you can list (immediately below your own number) an *alternative* number, where messages will be taken for you.

Be careful, however, to get permission from the people who will be taking your messages. And let them know the circumstances: Prospective employers will be calling to leave messages, and accuracy is *very* important.

You wouldn't want to call the wrong number or mispronounce a name given to you in error. Sometimes, well-meaning friends don't do well "under fire."

Making a Good Impression

Be *extremely* careful about the persons you select to take messages for you.

If your prospective employer calls that number and hears a sloppy, unintelligible voice that answers, "Yeah, who d'ya wanna talk to?" your prospective employer has every right to question your judgment or your choice of friends.

When calling a semifinalist for employment with the corporation for which I served as Corporate Director of Human Resources, the candidate's spouse answered.

The answering voice was very unprofessional, not businesslike, and there was excessive noise in the background: television and kids crying.

Prospective employers deserve a better impression of any candidate than this. Be careful. Or you may be rejected for reasons you never considered or which you thought would never count against you!

Writing Your Address and Phone Number(s)

Here are some samples of the ways you might want to write your phone numbers:

(502) 555-1546 (work)	(601) 555-4444 (home)
(502) 807-2116 (home)	(601) 711-6512 (parents' home, messages)
(409) 555-1212 (home)	(212) 555-6401 (home)
(409) 311-4400 (spouse's)	(212) 607-4400 (answering service) (business phone)

Considering all of the preceding advice, write your own name and address in the space below. Write this information just as you want it to appear on your resume. Remember, no abbreviations, and include your 9-digit ZIP code too:

_____

_____

Now, write your phone number(s), with area code, here:

(_____) _____ - _____
Area code   Number

(_____) _____ - _____
Area code   Number

▶Job Objective

Including a Job or Career Objective on your resume is a controversial topic.

If you use an objective, experts will tell you that you must be specific...say exactly what you do or what you're looking for. True!

But what if you have a *first-choice* career objective and would gladly accept a second-choice job, or even a third or fourth choice? If you list your first choice only, you will almost certainly be eliminated from consideration for any other opportunities.

So here's what I recommend: If you know what you want to do, very specifically, write a job or career objective. Stick to it. Hang in there. You'll get what you want eventually.

Don't Be Vague

But if you don't know what you want to do, don't write an objective at all.

You're better off not having one than having a vague, poorly written objective. Don't expect employers to be impressed with generalities; they won't be.

And neither will employers be able to make your career decisions for you. That's not their job. It's yours.

A competent, college-degreed professional wrote the following job objective at the top of the resume:

A challenging opportunity with a forward-looking organization, in one or more of the following areas: marketing, management, distribution, public relations, or personnel.

What's wrong? Too many options. This candidate looks indecisive. Another college graduate wrote this:

A challenging opportunity in management.

Sorry, fellow. You lose. This says *nothing,* other than "I don't know *what I want!"* It was written by a 45-year-old college graduate with over 15 years of business experience. He should have known better, but didn't.

His objective is simply too broad, too general, and meaningless. It hurts the applicant instead of helping him.

Most employers want to fill a specific job that requires specific skills. You really can't expect them to figure out the job for which you are qualified.

Your job objective, then, must also be specific. It should let the reader know, immediately, what job you are looking for. It should imply the types of problems you can *solve* and let them know that "you're the one"—or, at the very least, that you deserve further consideration.

Make Headlines

Think of a job objective as a headline. It will attract the reader, or it will not.

If your job objective says, in a few short words, that you will be able to solve one of the problems that exists in the organization, your chances are *good* for avoiding immediate rejection.

If it says *nothing* or is vague, too long, or indecisive, you're *out.* You're rejected in a 3-second glance—based on a job or career objective *alone,* before the reader even *sees* the body of your resume!

Here are some short, well-written job/career objectives:

- General Sales Manager for machine tool manufacturer
- Stockbroker

- Entry-level position in soft goods retailing
- Training program in retailing/ marketing management
- Assistant Buyer for giftware Representative
- Auto Mechanic
- Auto Mechanic for Porsche-Audi cars
- Travel Agent in agency using SABRE system
- Housekeeper/Supervisor for hotel or motel
- Life Insurance Sales/Investment Counselor

- Assistant Loan Officer, savings & loan association or bank
- Mechanical Engineer with manufacturing firm
- Sales Representative, floor covering retailer
- Territorial Sales Representative, appliance distributor/wholesaler
- Incentive/Premium Sales

- Marketing firm in Midwest
- Editorial Assistant in sports-related publishing
- Executive Secretary/ Administrative Assistant
- Word Processing Supervisor

Now, write your own job objective, based on the skills you have and want to use on the job:

_____

_____

_____

_____

_____

▶Education

If you are a recent graduate (of a university, college, career or business college, vocational school, community college, or any other substantial program), education *probably* belongs near the top of your resume.

This is especially true if the courses you studied have a direct relationship to the career you hope to enter.

But if you graduated years ago, or if your educational background does not relate to your present goals, you may want to list education items near the end of your resume.

Some of the examples that follow include more than the basics: they include also statements about courses taken, accomplishments, and extracurricular activities. This can be a good idea unless you decide to list this information elsewhere in your resume.

Here are some examples of recent college graduates:

- **Bachelor of Arts degree**
  St. Olaf's College (Northfield, Minnesota)
  Majors: Psychology and English
  Grade point average: 3.85/40
  Graduated "Magna cum Laude"
  June, 19XX

- **Bachelor of Science degree in Business Administration**
  University of Georgia
  Athens, Georgia
  Date of graduation: May, 19XX

If you have an advanced degree, list it first:

- **Master's degree in Guidance and Counseling**
  University of Southern California
  Los Angeles, California
  Graduation: December, 19XX
  Graduated with honors while working full-time. Includes one-year practicum with a variety of clients.
  Degree granted: June, 19XX

- **Master of Business Administration**
  The Kellogg School, Northwestern University
  Evanston, Illinois
  Upper 25 percent of Class. Started a student service business while going to school. Earned enough to pay tuition and expenses.
  Degree granted: June, 19XX

Examples of career or technical school graduates:

- **Associate degree in Electronic and Computer Science**
  Computer Institute of Pittsburgh
  Pittsburgh, Pennsylvania
  Date of graduation:
  December, 19XX
  Grade average: 3.65/4.0

  Courses include
  Calculus, physics
  AF & RF Analog Electronics
  Circuit Design & Fabrication
  Digital Electronics
  Microprocessors

Playing the Grade Game

What if you didn't do well in school? Must you put the information about education at the top? Must you admit to your low grades?

Of course not. The resume is a sales document, and if you use it correctly, it gets you *in*. It doesn't keep you *out*.

So you say those things that will make you look like a good candidate. If you have good grades, you list them. If not, omit them.

- **Acme Diesel Training Schools**
  Completed 2-year training program
  Certificate granted: December 19XX
  Grade average: B+ to A–
    Program included 12 months of on-the-job experience under the supervision of an experienced heavy-duty diesel mechanic

- **Institute of Business Careers**
  One-year program in Executive Secretary and Business Management, Certificate of Achievement, Leadership Award
  Graduated June, 19XX
  Courses include
    Computerized Accounting
    Office Management
    Business Communications
    Advanced Word Processing
    Systems & Procedures
    Time Management

Here are some ways to present your high school experience:

- **Shawnee Mission East High School**
  Prairie Village, Kansas
  Graduated with honors, June, 19XX
  College preparatory classes:
  GPA 3.8/4.0

- **Storm Lake Area High School**
  Storm Lake, Minnesota
  Class of 19XX: Active in varsity sports, class president

- **Denver Vocational High School**
  Denver, Colorado
  Business courses in accounting, word processing, data entry management, and others
  Date of graduation: June, 19XX

- **Edina High School**
  Edina, California
  Graduated with honors June, 19XX
  Elected to student government counsel twice

Or state that you "Received excellent grades in mathematics, drafting, and mechanics courses." Will the reader recognize that you are also omitting information about the poor grades you received in English Composition courses?

Possibly. But if your grades in significant courses were better than your overall average, you may prefer to use such a statement anyway.

If you have been out of school for many years, your grades are far less important than your performance in the jobs you have held.

If you want a dividing line to help you decide whether to include your grade point average (your GPA), choose 3.0 on a 4.0 system.

On the 4.0 system, the most common system used for grading in high schools and colleges in the United States, each A grade is given a weight of 4 points; a B receives 3 points, a C is 2 points, and a D is 1 point.

Someone who has all B's would have a 3.0 grade average; a straight-A student would have a 4.0 average.

Is a 2.5 grade average bad? No. But it is not good enough to include as a *plus* factor in a resume.

Winning the Grade Game

In my 10 years as a college placement director, almost *every* student who graduated found a job he or she wanted after graduation. But the easiest way I could sell a student to an employer was to say that he or she "has a 3.8 grade average," or he or she "has a 3.3 in his or her major."

Good grades are an almost certain ticket to getting in the door for an interview. The lower your grades or the poorer your record, the more doors you may have to knock on to get a chance at the job you want.

And the harder you'll have to work to make an impression in the interview.

If students only knew how much good grades impress a prospective employer, they would surely put more effort toward achieving better grades.

I've never heard a mediocre student say that he or she had "done my very best work all the time." Almost invariably, they say, instead, that "I know I could have done better if I had worked harder."

(If you are reading this in time to make a difference in your grades and make a change in your habits—*do it now!*)

Listing Your Educational Experience

Here are some tips before you begin.

List the names of all the schools from which you graduated, beginning with your high school. If you did not graduate, list the last school you attended and the year in which you would have graduated, such as "Class of 1989."

If you attended four high schools, list only the one from which you received your diploma. The same is true for colleges and universities. List the one from which you graduated or the school you attended most recently.

Most colleges and high schools include you as an alumnus (male) or alumna (female) even if you did not graduate. Employers are interested in just knowing that you *did* attend or that you *did* graduate.

They are not as interested in knowing each school you may have attended while moving from city to city, or while changing your mind about what subjects to study.

Here, as elsewhere in your resume, do not use abbreviations. Spell out the names of organizations—even streets and locations, and spell them correctly. Begin by completing the following form for your most recent educational experience.

MOST RECENT EDUCATIONAL EXPERIENCE

School name: _____

Location (city and state): _____

Note: Street addresses, ZIP codes, and phone numbers are not required here. Be prepared to provide this information, if asked, to an employer needing to check your references or credentials.

Degree/Diploma/Certificate awarded, if any: _____

_____

Month and year of graduation: _____

Courses that directly relate to the job you are seeking: _____

_____

_____

_____

Class rank: I ranked _____ in a class of _____ graduating students.
I had a grade average _____ out of a possible _____. [and/or]
I had a grade average of _____ in my major subjects of study, out of a possible _____.

Special skills you acquired, accomplishments, honors, projects, extracurricular or related activities: _____

_____

_____

_____

Note: Use additional sheets of paper as needed to list all your related activities and accomplishments. But, before you write your resume, select the top few things you feel are most important for an employer to know.

Now, for each school you attended or from which you graduated, list the information required on the form that follows.

SCHOOL INFORMATION

School name: _____

Location (city & state): _____

_____

Degree/Diploma/Certificate awarded, if any: _____

_____

Month and year of graduation: _____

Courses that directly relate to the job you are seeking: _____

_____

_____

_____

_____

_____

Class rank: I ranked _____ in a class of _____ graduating students.
I had a grade average of _____ out of a possible _____. [and/or]
I had a grade average of _____ in my major subjects of study, out of a possible _____.

Special skills you acquired, accomplishments, honors, projects, and extracurricular or related activities: _____

_____

_____

_____

_____

There you have it. A record of your educational experiences.

In the next chapter, I will show you the sections of a resume that *really* get the attention of most employers.

I'm qualified

Chapter 3
Tell 'Em What Sells 'Em

Your past experiences are the most important part of your resume. An employer is going to pay you for these experiences, in the hope that they will directly translate into skills valuable to the employer.

Past experiences indicate how you are likely to perform in the future. So you'll want to present your strongest experiences in a clear and powerful way.

Why Are They Looking to Hire You—or Anyone?

When anyone buys something, the person is often buying more than the product or service itself. The individual buys the *benefits,* the specific features, advantages, and attributes that the product or service will bring.

When you buy a television, for example, you are buying more than the hardware. You are buying the following:

- Design
- Convenience features (remote channel changing, muting, etc.)
- Reputation for quality and reliability
- Picture quality
- Lifestyle benefits

Charles Revlon, the famed founder of the Revlon cosmetics empire, was fond of saying, "I don't sell cosmetics, I sell hope." In a similar way an employer, too, buys the *benefits* a job applicant brings to the organization.

You'll want to pay special attention, then, to the ways you can best communicate your skills, talents, abilities, and aptitudes that you can bring to an organization—the *benefits* you offer.

The more benefits you bring, and the fewer potential problems, the more likely you are to be screened *in* and not screened *out*.

In your resume, the best way to accomplish this is *to do what most people neglect to do:*

- Emphasize your *accomplishments,* and
- Tell the reader any *specific results* you have had.

This is far better than listing the "duties and responsibilities of the job," which is what most people do in resumes.

They fail to *market* themselves. Employers buy *results, accomplishments, and benefits.* So, that's what you should put in your resume!

►What Are Accomplishments?

Accomplishments are things you started, completed, worked on, created, developed, or made possible...things that happened because *you* were there!

An accomplishment can be a long- or short-term project, something created or supervised by others, or by yourself.

But they are always specific, not general, and they are always things in which you played an active role (even if others worked with you.)

Look at the difference between a duty (which does *not* market you effectively but is the way most people write their resumes) and the same situation described as an accomplishment:

A duty:

Wrote weekly reports on sales and submitted these to home office.

An accomplishment:

Completed 156 summary reports on sales, including weekly volume, percent of increase, new clients seen. Received commendation from sales manager for accuracy and for never missing a deadline.

Which, do you think, will impress an employer more?

►What about Results?

Doing something is one thing; doing it well is quite a different thing. Results detail the positive differences, advantages, and changes that occurred as a consequence of your efforts. They are best expressed in easy-to-understand words or in numbers.

When writing your resume, select the statistics that *best* show the results you have achieved and, therefore, the kinds of results you are capable of achieving for an employer.

Here is an "ordinary" result (*not* a good example):

Sold complete line of cars and trucks for a major metropolitan dealer for six years. Interfaced with sales force, customers, service department; prospected by phone.

Now, look at how this same experience can be changed into a *good* statement:

- Member, "Winner's Circle," honors sales club for Goodman Chevrolet, 1987-1989.
- Sold 200+ new cars and 50+ new trucks annually—over $2,500,000 in sales—for each of the past four years.
- Received dealer's highest measured customer rating for most of the 70 months on sales force.
- Averaged 50 cold call phone contacts daily, converting 6 percent into customers.
- Contacted "prior dealership customers" list by phone and set new sales records with this previously ignored group.

Which of these descriptions would impress you the most?

▶ The RAQ System (Pronounced "Rack")

Here's a great secret. Few resume writers or readers know how powerful it can be. The easy way to remember it is to call it "The RAQ System."

R	for	**Results!**
A	for	**Accomplishments!**
Q	for	**Quantify!**

To ensure that you create a marketable resume, make RAQ *your* system.

Rather than create a laundry list of everything you did—every task, every project, every committee, every *everything*—for a particular employer, distill each job down to *specific results!* Combine several things into one phrase or sentence, if you like, but distill it down into a 1-2-3 line sentence that *tells what happened* as a *result* of your efforts, or as a result of the efforts of a group in which you participated. If you merely say what you did, or what you were responsible for, your resume will read like 90 percent of the other resumes...and that's what you *don't* want.

Numbers have a hidden psychological advantage too. They tend to be more believable than "just words." If you're willing to reveal actual numbers rather than just concepts, it seems as if you are a person who tells the truth.

What we just said is this:

Employers want to know what *results* you attained while you were there...not "all the things you did." Numbers do that easily and well.

Write phrases containing numbers in a format that emphasizes your results as *accomplishments.* Give yourself credit where credit is due: to you yourself.

Finally, **whenever you can**—and that is in *many more* situations than you might initially think—**QUANTIFY!**

Look at every single result or accomplishment you've written.

Then ask yourself, "How can I quantify this? How can I put it into numbers or a percentage of increase? What were the estimated savings over the prior year? How many programs did I write? How many hours were saved? How many? How many? How many?

Don't simply say that you "trained personnel." How many? How many training sessions did you conduct annually? Monthly?

Don't just say that you were "appointed supervisor." How many full-time people did you supervise? How many part-time?

Supervised 7 full-time and 13 part-time clerks and stockers; held 50+ training sessions annually and improved set-up time efficiencies by more than 17%. Estimated annual savings exceeded $8,000.

In resumes, you can, and should, use Arabic numbers rather than write out the words; 23% or **$14 million dollars** or **$14,000,000** are all easier to read, and more impressive, than writing out "twenty-three percent" or "fourteen million dollars."

Let your common sense prevail. If you supervised only two people, you might want to omit the number 2 and instead say that you were "selected as supervisor over other employees after only 3 months." Both are true, but the latter sounds much better.

▶ Analyze Your Work Experience

Your previous work experience is an important source of resume content. More recent experience is of greater importance than examples from years ago.

If you are young, or if your previous jobs are unrelated to your current objective, the *type* of experience you have is not all that important to most employers.

Employers are more interested in the fact that you worked somewhere, that you are ambitious, and that you worked hard and did a good job than they are in what sort of job you had—unless it has a very specific relationship to the job you are seeking.

But your advancement at McDonald's to supervisor or your ability to train new staff could well add to your attractiveness as a candidate with virtually any employer.

And so could the fact that you supervised six employees. Or that you earned funds for 80 percent of your schooling expenses while maintaining a B average.

So whether you are 20 and just starting out or 45 with considerable work experience, you want your resume to show off your accomplishments in the best possible light.

So, let's get on with it.

▶ The Basics: Selling Your Work Experience

I have constructed a worksheet later in this section to help organize your work experiences. Here are some tips for completing it:

The Organization. For each employer, write the full name of the company (spelled correctly) and the city and state where it is located.

Title. Write your job title. If your job title is difficult to understand or if it doesn't mean anything by itself, change it!

- Change "Sales Associate" to "Senior Retail Sales Clerk, Men's Clothing Department," if that is appropriate.

- Change "Secretary" to "Office Manager" if that description is more accurate.

City and State/Province. If the job was located in a suburb of a major city, it is OK to use that city's name.

Length of Employment. Give the month and year you began, and the month and year that you left. If you are still employed there, write "present" in the appropriate place.

Results and Accomplishments. Write *short* statements of specific results and accomplishments you had on this job.

Use Action Words

Begin each statement with an action verb. Use words or ideas from the "Action Words" list that follows to make sure you begin each phrase with an action word.

Write each statement as a *phrase,* not a *sentence.*

• Accomplished	• Directed	• Inspected	• Presented
• Achieved	• Drove	• Instructed	• Produced
• Adjusted	• Encouraged	• Interviewed	• Promoted
• Administered	• Enlarged	• Invented	• Protected
• Analyzed	• Entertained	• Judged	• Recorded
• Built	• Equipped	• Justified	• Reduced
• Compared	• Established	• Led	• Reorganized
• Compiled	• Evaluated	• Made	• Replaced
• Composed	• Exhibited	• Maintained	• Reported
• Conducted	• Fabricated	• Managed	• Researched
• Constructed	• Figured	• Mixed	• Revised
• Controlled	• Graded	• Motivated	• Served
• Counseled	• Guided	• Moved	• Sold
• Created	• Handled	• Negotiated	• Supervised
• Cut	• Headed	• Operated	• Taught
• Designated	• Implemented	• Organized	• Tended
• Designed	• Improved	• Persuaded	• Trained
• Determined	• Increased	• Planned	• Won
• Developed	• Initiated	• Prepared	• Wrote
• Devised			

Omit these three words from your writings: "I," "me," and "my." Then omit three more: "a," "an," and "the." These are "extra" words, and they are not particularly appropriate for resume writing. Your phrases will be cleaner, shorter, and easier to understand if you omit these words.

Describe each accomplishment separately. If you think about it, you may be able to separate one project into several smaller skills or accomplishments. This can give you shorter (and more powerful) statements rather than a description of one big project.

Keep each accomplishment short so that it can be read *quickly* by the reader!

Use numbers whenever you can—exact numbers or percentages are powerful.

And if you had several jobs or accomplishments that sound the same, *do not* repeat the same thing for each job or department in which you worked. This should be obvious, but I have seen it hundreds of times!

Here are some examples of "good" statements:

- Wrote 300+ programs for IBM mainframe computer system.

- Received seven letters of commendation from sales executives for exceeding quotas.

- Increased sales 41 percent over prior year for same territory. Established 77 new accounts.

- Implemented new sales record system, saving 4 hours weekly for each sales representative, or total of 128 weekly hours, which were then available for sales calls.

- Managed sales force of 36 independent agents and 22 company sales representatives, covering 7 fields and 29 territories.

- Reduced inventories 17 percent by developing and implementing new sales forecasting system.

- Reformulated 13 cereal and snack products to conform with federal guidelines for shelf-life improvement.

- Reformulated nondairy topping product for improved taste. Decreased cost of raw materials by $150,000 annually.

- Invented and patented new method of treating perishable food products. Reduced annual cost of formulation by more than $250,000 per year.

- Negotiated and sold injection molding division for parent company. Resulted in $3,000,000 profit; saved plant shutdown costs estimated at $170,000.

- Supervised 7 full-time and 18 part-time retail sales employees.

- Won 14 design awards for graphic design of three metals-industry magazines published for nationwide distribution.

- Developed new typesetting system using MS-DOS computer system when software was not available to meet company's needs.

- Won ADDY Award for excellence in creativity for full-page newspaper advertisement. National award was won by only 3 people from 7,000 entries.

Do this for "each" job you have held. It may seem like a great deal of work, but do it in a relaxed environment, while watching TV or listening to your favorite relaxing music, and the words will come quickly.

Use additional sheets of paper to describe your various jobs as needed, using the worksheet that follows:

WORK EXPERIENCE WORKSHEET

Employer: _____

Job title: _____

Address: _____

Employed from: (month/year) _____ to: (month/year) _____

Results and accomplishments: _____

_____

_____

_____

_____

_____

_____

WORK EXPERIENCE WORKSHEET

Employer: _____

Job title: _____

Address: _____

Employed from: (month/year) _____ to: (month/year) _____

Results and accomplishments: _____

_____

_____

_____

_____

_____

_____

▶ After You Have Documented Your Work Experience

After you have completed a worksheet for each of your jobs, decide which *one* result or accomplishment was *most* important in each one. Which would look *best* to a future employer?

Rank that result or accomplishment #1. Choose the next most important. Rank it #2. And so on.

If you did the same things on each of your last several jobs, do this: For the jobs you held years ago, write shorter job/results/accomplishments paragraphs than you write for more recent jobs.

Reword the group of related accomplishments to sound slightly different, and use shorter statements. If some results (expressed in numbers, percentages) and increases are significant, be sure to include some of these in your statements.

Generally, the more recent your job, the more space it should receive on your resume. Jobs you held 10 or more years ago are usually *considerably* less significant.

If these "older" jobs do not relate at all to the job you are now seeking, they deserve only a line or two. Mention them primarily to show where you were working and for how long.

You will see, when you finish writing each statement, that some are more important than others. And that some relate more directly to the work you want now.

This process will help you begin thinking about which items to include in your final resume, and which ones to eliminate.

For most people, the work experience section of their resume is the most important. You are hired for the *results* you have had on your jobs, for your *accomplishments,* and for your *ability* to *solve employer problems.*

In the statements in this section, you are explaining why you will be a valuable employee. The reader is more likely to consider you favorably because of these statements than from anything else in your resume.

This is generally true unless you are relatively young.

For most young people, "meaningful work, related to what you want to do for a career" is difficult to find. So don't be discouraged if this section, for you, is filled with results and accomplishments from your after-school grocery-bagging experiences, your baby-sitting jobs, and such.

These jobs still give employers an idea of your accomplishments, of the responsibilities you have been given, and of any promotions you have earned or awards you have won.

▶ Personal Accomplishments

There is more to life than work. Many times, things you have accomplished outside of work can be just as impressive to an employer as work-related activities. These external accomplishments can be particularly important if you have only limited work experience.

Complete the following sections for each period in your life to help review this part of your experience.

High School. List any clubs, societies, athletic teams, or other organizations you were involved in and any awards or accomplishments for them.

_____

_____

_____

_____

_____

_____

18-22 years old. List any clubs, societies, athletic teams, or other organizations you were involved in and any awards or accomplishments for them.

_____

_____

_____

_____

_____

_____

_____

22-25 years old. List any clubs, societies, athletic teams, or other organizations you were involved in and any awards or accomplishments for them.

_____

_____

_____

_____

_____

_____

25 years old and above. List any clubs, societies, athletic teams, or other organizations you were involved in and any awards or accomplishments for them.

_____
_____
_____
_____
_____
_____

▶Choose Your Most Impressive Results

Now, from all these, choose the _most_ impressive results and accomplishments you have had in your extracurricular, community, and social life.

Choose significant items, just as you did when you listed accomplishments from your work experiences.

Place #1 alongside the most impressive or significant item. Do the same for #2, #3, and so forth.

Now, in order, list the extracurricular statements in the following spaces. Again, use the action language you used when you wrote about your work accomplishments.

Here are some examples for you to follow:

- Elected President of Student Council for 1,700-student high school by widest margin in school history.
- Developed and chaired project to raise $4,500 for school veterans' memorial.
- Elected Captain, swim team; won four varsity letters; set two team speed records.
- Elected Secretary-Treasurer of Girls' Athletic Association two consecutive years.
- Represented church youth group at national delegate convention; served on Credentials Committee.
- Worked at several restaurants part-time during high school and college; earned funds for 75 percent of college expenses.
- Selected as female romantic lead for three high school musicals; received excellent reviews from local papers.
- Received Regional Musical Awards for piano; studied piano privately for nine years; choir accompanist.
- Elected Honored Queen, Bethel #6, Job's Daughters; increased membership 27 percent during term of office 1992-93.

- Selected for membership, Rotary Club of Downtown Phoenix, 1993. Plan to serve on education and scholarship committees.
- President, Scottsdale Jaycees, 1993-94; raised $8,000 for Special Olympics.
- Elected Lieutenant Governor, Arizona Boys State, 1989; led legislative session.

How many of these "Honors, Awards, and Achievements" should you include? Some people, even some "resume experts" might say that you should omit them entirely.

I disagree.

If a potential employer has any doubt about you as a possible candidate, these achievements may be the very thing that will tilt the odds in your favor.

Indeed, a study of corporate personnel representatives who recruit graduating seniors on college campuses showed that participation in activities, offices, and organizations indicated that *leadership potential* was the #1 reason for choosing final candidates.

Now, in order, list the honors, awards, and achievements you want to include in your resume:

_____   _____
_____   _____
_____   _____
_____   _____
_____   _____

▶ Think Again

If you don't have any activities, honors, awards, or extracurricular accomplishments, don't feel left out.

First, you probably *do* have some. Think again. Think about how you may have spent your free time. Think about a boss who may have paid you a special compliment about your work, your effort, or your dependability.

You might include this in a section rarely used, but possibly useful.

▶ What Others Say

A short, swift compliment may be just the thing to compensate for your lack of "honors." If your boss once said that you were her best employee, use the words she said.

Best employee I've ever had in fourteen years of hiring high school students.

—*Linda Keeler, Manager, 7-Eleven store*
East Dubuque

Or if a teacher once said that your assignments were always handed in on time, repeat that teacher's words:

I admire your neat work and the fact that you always have assignments in on time.

—*Allen B. Molitor, Teacher, American History*
Darien High School

If you use quotations, be sure they are accurate! And keep them short. One phrase or sentence is usually enough! You want employers to read it, absorb it, and then generalize from it.

What you want them to remember is this:

He seems like a good person, and other people think so too.

▶ Special Skills

This is the place to list any special skills not already covered in your Work Experience or Education sections. Such skills might include typing, operating specific machinery and equipment, and so on.

Make a list of any special skills you might have that would interest an employer. And mark the ones that you want to use in a job.

Maybe you can type but would rather not let employers know this (for fear of being labeled a secretary—when you really want to be a management trainee).

There's no law that says you must use *all* your skills in a job. Or admit to them on a resume.

List any of these skills in the following spaces:

_____

_____

_____

_____

_____

_____

▶ Personal Information

In years past, this information was expected. People who were reading resumes looked for it. But times change, and so do resume customs.

Omit information such as date of birth or age, place of birth, family information, marital status, health, height, and weight.

Put in anything here that might help you, and leave out anything that could hurt you. Although this section can be left off your resume completely, it *might* be helpful to include some things that do support your ability to do the job but don't fit anywhere else on your resume.

Condition of your health, in one word: _____.

(I recommend the word "excellent.")

Have you traveled much? Where? List the unusual or interesting regions, states, or foreign countries you've visited:

_____

_____

_____

_____

_____

Have you had any special training or professional schooling, attended intensive seminars, or gone to service/military schools that are applicable to the civilian job you're hoping to land?

List them here, including the length of each course.

_____

_____

_____

_____

_____

What are your hobbies? Interests? List them here. (Some ideas: playing baseball, composing classical music for piano, collecting first day stamp issues, reading about current business trends, making your own clothes, working on cars, skydiving, parasailing, writing movie reviews for local paper, eating out, seeing foreign films, volunteering at local nursing home, assisting Sunday School teachers, exploring 35 mm photography, scripting and videotaping original variety shows, building bookcases, making needle-point pictures, etc.)

Now, start looking at, and thinking about, which ones of the above you would like to have a prospective employer know about? Which ones might make you look more attractive to an employer? Which ones would not?

Some kinds of personal information can cause problems. In most cases, your resume should be free of references to your political, religious, or philosophical beliefs.

An exception to this general rule might be when you are applying to a religious, political, or philosophical organization. Degrees from religious colleges or universities, therefore, might be helpful if you are applying to work at a hospital run by that religion. People of all religions may work there, of course, but you might have a slight advantage.

Political preferences are no reason for selecting one applicant over another. Your beliefs are your own business as long as you don't try to force them on other employees in the organization.

But listing that you were a member of the Young Democrats when the chances are 50-50 that the reader will be a Republican wouldn't seem to be a smart idea. You'd be better off eliminating the reference entirely. Or, you might say "Elected President of political organization with membership of 80" instead of identifying the Young Democrats specifically.

Use this as a guideline: if you feel that any of this personal information is to your advantage in the job hunt, you *may* use it if you want.

I recommend a short statement, under a category titled "PERSONAL INFORMATION," very close to the end of your resume, if you use such information at all. Here are some examples:

- Excellent health, no serious illnesses
- Middle child of five children; father is airline sales representative; mother is office manager for plumbing firm
- Married to Ralph, computer engineer, for 27 years; raised five children
- Have traveled widely throughout United States, Canada, and Europe; enjoy travel photography
- Enjoy sewing clothes, working on church committees, and doing volunteer work at nursing home

▶ References

References are not usually listed on a resume.

A resume is one of the first things an employer sees in the hiring process; reference calls and inquiries aren't made until later. But you might begin now to think about which people you would choose to recommend you, to inform the prospective employer about such things as your trustworthiness, honesty, dependability, work diligence and habits, career goals, quality of your work, and even the kinds of friends you have.

The best choices for references are usually, but need not always be, people who have watched you work, supervised your work, instructed you, graded you, and who have seen you progress to new levels of competence. Who are these people? Usually your teachers, bosses, supervisors, owners of businesses or executives of organizations where you have worked, and with whom you have had a direct working relationship.

References may be requested from others: ministers, neighbors, or your family doctor or attorney. But these are not considered as valuable by most employers. Obviously, if you were applying for a job with a church, a reference from your pastor might prove to be very important. But for a job as Administrative Assistant for the Vice President of Manufacturing, a minister's comments might not be as significant.

Put some of their names down now, and then think about how you might approach these people to ask their permission to act as a reference for you.

When you select the people to be your references, you will choose about three or four. For each of these you will need the following information:

- Full name
- Name of organization
- Address
- City, state, ZIP
- Job title of the person
- Your working or personal relationship, in a few words at most
- Telephone number, including area code

Remember, references are not required on your resume because it represents an early stage in the application process. Your goal now is to create a resume which is so attractive that you will be asked to come in for an interview. After a successful interview, if you are under final consideration as a candidate, the employer will ask for your references. If you want to forget about references entirely, or if you hope the employer does, a simple phrase like one of the following will often do nicely:

Business and personal references are available and will be furnished on request.

Excellent business and personal references are available.

Complete business and personal references are available and will gladly be furnished on request.

Well, you get the picture by now. Except to say that such a statement can just as easily be left off the resume entirely. Because it really says nothing.

And one other thing, *always* ask permission before using a person as a reference. Talk over with each one what the person will say in advance, and use a name *only* if the person will say good things about you.

An Added List of References

Some resumes have a "List of References for William Smith" as an addendum to the regular resume. Is this OK?

If someone or some organization has specifically asked you to submit a resume because a particular person knows you, or because the individual knows your reputation through someone else or from a consultant who knows you, then it's *an excellent idea!*

If someone has called or written and requested that you submit a resume, the organization has a predetermined interest in you. And if a company might spend $1,200 in air fare, hotel, and other expenses to interview you, the presence of references and phone numbers will be a convenience to those interested in you; they'd probably prefer to make a few phone calls to inquire about you before committing to spending the $1,200 on you.

But how about "just sending the list of references with the resume?" Go ahead, if you want. It can't hurt. But as you read a few moments ago, most firms use references toward the end of the interview process, just before an offer is extended. Sending an addendum now is just another way of saying "People seem to like me and are willing to say so. I get along well with others. I'm open and honest and willing to have you check me out."

The list in an addendum might look like this:

List of References for Brett A. Christopher

Mr. William B. Settles
Minister, First Community Church
5634 Osceola Drive
San Diego, California 92106-8864
(619) 555-9567; Fax (619) 555-9570
My pastor for 18 years

Mr. John W. Blair
President
KPYG-TV, Channel 28
12840 Mission Bay Boulevard
La Jolla, California 92119-5540
(619) 555-5300, ext. 450; Fax (619) 555-5399
My immediate sales manager for 5 years

Mr. Russell Daniels
Director, Marketing Internship Program
San Diego State University
6632 Hyacinth Drive
San Diego, California 92108-3351
(619) 555-2318; Fax (619) 555-2320
My internship coordinator and supervisor

How many names should you provide? Because employers have just as much trouble as you and I do reaching people by phone in one call, you should include six to eight complete names, titles if any, complete addresses, phone numbers, extensions, FAX numbers, and a short phrase saying how you know the person, your working or personal relationship, etc.

Letters of Reference

Many organizations no longer give out references over the phone. They may even fear a lawsuit based on something they might say. Or they don't want to offend anyone. Supervisors sometimes resign from where you worked for other jobs. So getting a *written* letter of reference is becoming more and more important. This is the only way to be certain of getting a reference from a previous employer.

Not all references are good ones. How do you get a good reference?

From an employer's point of view, the best references are from those who can tell them the truth about your *performance,* not just that you are "a nice person."

Current and ex-bosses, as well as current teachers and ex-teachers, are probably the best people to do this. Your aunt, minister, dentists, and others who know you only as a friend, client, or relative are not acceptable references to an employer.

Begin by selecting some people who know your work and who will say positive things about you. Then help them in saying what you want them to say in their letters.

Remember, employers will be looking for negative information. Faint praise in a letter of reference can be damaging. So if you're asking someone to write a letter for you, be specific. *Tell* them what to say!

Tell them to write about specific accomplishments you were involved with, how vital your actions and results became to the organization, and so on.

Here are a few examples:

Amy was always dependable and on time. She got along extremely well with her coworkers, and we hate to see her resign and move away. Her work has been exceptional, and we would hire her again for this job or a more responsible one.

Bob was one of our hardest working students. He always did his home-work and was active in many extracurricular activities. He did all this while working to pay his tuition.

Don't be afraid to suggest improvements in the letter.

Or, if they say they'd love to give you a letter but they hate to write, offer to write something for them.

Ask them what they would say if they did write something. Then put it into words that make you sound like a trustworthy person and a good candidate.

And have them sign the letter if they agree with what you've said. On their letterhead. That helps convince an employer that your letters of reference are legitimate and reliable.

Offer to type the letter right away and have them sign it. Or you can draft the letter and have them type it on their letterhead right away.

If you walk out of the person's office with just their promise to write a letter "sometime soon," you may have a long wait.

Overcoming Bad References

Bad references can ruin everything! Good resumes, the perfect interview, excellent background—all can go down the tubes when your ex-boss says, "I wouldn't hire that guy again after what he did to me."

If you know or believe you have bad references, you have two options:

- Keep applying and hope you find someone who'll hire you without checking references at all. (Some smaller firms may not check references. Larger organizations have often been burned by hiring bad people and almost always check references to avoid being burned again.)

- Do something that turns those bad references into good ones.

This later option may be difficult. But it can be done!

Almost all wounds heal in time. It's a matter of "who eats the crow."

If it's a standoff—and both of you are unwilling to swallow your pride and make overtures to settle the hard feelings—remember *you* are the one who has the most to lose.

So YOU should take that first step toward a truce. Think of some *good* things about your ex-boss or your ex-company. Then send a letter, outlining those good things and thanking them for the good experience you had while you worked there.

Be positive. And don't reopen old wounds.

If you prefer, use the telephone instead of a letter. And say the same kinds of things.

Use truthful, positive comments and compliments—ones which will help the person understand that you want to patch things up and at least not be enemies from now on.

This technique often turns bad references into good ones.

And whenever you leave a job, or after you leave, do *yourself* a favor: *don't complain about anything.*

Not your boss.

Or the "rotten way" the company is run.

Or the "lousy pay" you were getting.

Smile. Swallow your pride.

Compliment your boss. And the company.

And pretend everything is wonderful.

Even if it isn't.

You'll only hurt yourself if you do otherwise. You will only make it difficult (if not impossible) to get good references when you need them.

And you *will* need them when you're looking for a job!

Using Testimonials in Your Resume

People are naturally skeptical. You may safely assume that most employers wonder if you're a "fake product" and "not likely to work after we buy your services."

One way to avoid this skepticism is to use the advertisers' favorite technique for dispelling doubt: the testimonial.

If several people are willing to tell how terrific you are, how effective a worker you are—and if these testimonials are readily available—these might turn the tide in your favor.

So, consider including testimonials in your resume! Edit them down to short punchy statements. They might be just the thing that sets you apart from your competitors.

How to get them?

- From reviews or evaluations of your work in your personnel file
- From documents, letters you have
- Letters from friends
- Letters from teachers/professors
- Letters from employers
- Letters from coworkers

If you don't have any such letters, ask for them! Consider these examples. You can include these at the beginning or end of the resume (wherever they would have the most impact):

As our night attendant for Bill's Chevron Service, Sally Kobe performed her work in an outstanding way. We entrusted her with all our equipment and gave her responsibility for making bank deposits and locking the store at 11 p.m. We were never disappointed in her and recommend her highly as a dependable, loyal employee.

—William Kozlicki, Owner

This statement could be shortened as follows:

Sally Kobe is a dependable, loyal employee.

> *—William Kozlicki, Owner, Bill's Chevron Service*

Here are other examples:

Walter Upchurch worked for our insurance agency for three years while he attended classes at Clark County Community College. He typed all our policy claim forms and did our company payroll and bookkeeping. His work has always been of excellent quality, and we are especially pleased with his dependability, including his attendance (he never missed a day!).

> *—William Liebert, CLU, Liebert Insurance Agency*

Bill Gallant is the finest young man I've ever known. He is an excellent youth leader and sets an example for all the kids to follow. I'd like my own kids to grow up to be like Bill.

> *—Jeff Parker, Director, Springfield YMCA*

Jennifer Johnson was my outstanding student this year. She did her work on time, and it was always of excellent quality. She received one of three A's I awarded, but hers was tops in the class. I'd teach forever if all the students were like Jennifer.

> *—Todd Bogwell, Assistant Professor, Midwest University*

Our Student Ambassadors are carefully selected to be the best possible representatives of the college. Among these, the best performer and worker is usually elected President. This year, it is Patrick Ryan, and Pat has outdone himself. In my memory, Pat is the best of the best.

> *—Ronald Zess, Faculty Advisor*

My service station is more than my job. It is the key to my career and to my family life as well. A good employee at my station is someone who not only works for me, but also is a good representative for my business. If I get a bad guy, my kids may not go to college. John Clark is the perfect employee: trustworthy, dependable, always neatly groomed, and pleasant. My customers enjoy coming in and usually ask for John. I recommend him highly.

> *—Alice Springs, Owner, Springs Service*

Do you have some testimonials like these? If not, can you get some? From past employers? Or coworkers? Or teachers? Or friends?

If you do not have letters of reference, plan on getting them as soon as possible. If you do, summarize some of the best statements here for possible use in your resume later.

Testimonial statements:

_____

_____

_____

_____

_____

_____

_____

_____

_____

_____

_____

_____

_____

_____

_____

_____

_____

_____

_____

_____

Chapter 4
Designing an Outstanding Resume

Tailor Your Resume for Excellence

Now that you've gathered information about yourself, you're ready to begin putting your resume together.

Unless you are now prepared to invest enough time to research, write, edit, and then do the final copy of a resume that will make an *excellent* impression on the reader, all this work will have been in vain. Your resume is unlikely to be noticed or even glanced at, let alone read. One draft won't do it!

You will want to *tailor* your resume to what the reader *wants to read*—not necessarily what you want to say about yourself.

Too many people fail to put themselves in the reader's shoes! They see the resume as an opportunity to report everything about their history, because it makes them feel good to talk about all the things they've done.

The reader is looking for a *capsule impression* of you in a quick read-through of your resume. If you bury the essentials in a sea of words, the reader will never find them.

▶The Eye-Strain Approach

Here is an example of bad resume writing:

September 1989 — June 1990 SAFETY REPRESENTATIVE

Responsibilities: Coordinate and administer the safety, accident prevention, housekeeping, sanitation, and other related programs as assigned. Investigate accidents and supervise the preparation of accident reports and statistical summaries; review claims for worker's compensation. Check buildings, facilities, fire prevention systems, storage of dangerous fluids and gases, material handling equipment, etc, to ensure compliance with mandatory regulations and insurance requirements. Establish, coordinate, and maintain Company Fire Brigade. Study, plan, and formulate new and revised safety programs and rules; prepare recommendations and implement conformance with those which meet approval. Coordinate activities with Worker's Compensation Insurance Carrier. Select and approve purchase of standard manufactured safety services or design; expedite construction and installation of machine guards and point of operation safety.

If you were a busy employer, would you want to read this? Of course not!

The resume is *not* a place where you outline your job description or list every single duty you had. It is a place to highlight experiences that *will be relevant to the reader's requirements*—not to stroke your ego.

This isn't the place to say, "I'm wonderful." This is the place to highlight significant *results* and *accomplishments* from your experience.

To describe yourself in terms of the results you had on the job. The things you accomplished. The effects you had on corporate profitability or organizational effectiveness. The sales increases you directly brought about.

In other words, the *provable* things.

To say "bright, witty, and intellectually gifted" shows only that you have a good opinion of yourself.

We all need to love ourselves and be aware of our good qualities. But putting these things in a resume comes off as arrogant.

Better that the reader should conclude such things from the accomplishments you describe.

Or hear it from others when they check your references.

▶Edit, Edit, Edit

You will eventually edit your first draft, edit the information down to a second draft (leaving out irrelevant information), edit down to a third draft (seeking better, more powerful, *shorter* words), edit down to a fourth draft (striving for grammatical perfection), and finally a fifth draft (adjusting the arrangement on the page). This will be your final preprinter copy.

In your fifth draft, you will also decide the *order* of your categories because you will want to highlight your *best* qualifications *early* in the resume.

Thus, if your strongest point is fifteen years of experience in the field in which you are applying for a job, your work experience will be more important than your education and should come before it.

But if you are a new graduate with little relevant experience, you will probably want to place your education before your work experience.

If you are a graduating student and a leader in clubs and athletics, but your grades aren't so good, you might want to highlight "Honors, Awards, and Achievements" within your educational background.

▶How Long Should Your Resume Be?

Most experts will tell you that your resume should be one page only—or two pages at the most.

And they are probably right because no one wants to read more than that.

Your job is to edit, edit, edit your resume. And then edit some more until your resume is a manageable, tight length.

This does not mean that you should scrunch your resume into one page (or two) just because this is the rule.

I've seen resumes that are two and a half pages long (or even three) *with lots of white space* that were better (easier to read) than two-pagers with too much copy.

It's better to have a *well-designed* resume that will get *read,* even if it is longer than a crowded resume.

If your resume is more than two pages long, the chances are that you're refusing to edit out irrelevant material in your background. Keep the resume to one or two pages, and you should be safe.

The best length for your resume depends on your experience. Students and recent graduates may have little difficulty producing their resume on one page.

Even if you have many years of experience, remember that jobs from many years ago deserve little (if any) space unless they are *really* special or prestigious, or truly relate somehow to the job you're trying to get now. And if nothing else you've done since then relates to that objective.

That would be a rare circumstance! So keep editing critically. Keep your resume short and easy to scan.

▶Secrets of Readability

When you find yourself in a bookstore, you probably flip casually through a book that interests you.

Why? You want to see if it's readable. Is it a book you will be able to read or *want* to read?

Is there good use of white space? Graphics? Are the paragraphs short? Or what?

For whatever reasons, this book must have looked inviting to you—*readable.* The same is true with resumes!

The first requirement of your resume is that it must be *inviting to the eye.* If it isn't, *it won't even get read!*

The potential resume reader (just like the potential book reader) looks at the following things:

- Are the sentences short? With easy or short words?
- Is there adequate spacing between lines?
- Are there many short one-sentence or two-sentence paragraphs? (If the words, sentences, and paragraphs are long, involved, and uninviting, no one will read them.)

Scholarly articles, academic journals, and most textbooks are written in a way that invites serious study. It takes concentration and effort to absorb the information in these kinds of writing.

Leisure writing, consumer magazine articles, newspapers, and advertising copy are written differently. Their authors know that readers of such things *will not have the time for serious study.*

So it is with your resume. You've got *one chance.*

Think now about the leisure reading *you* do. What does it *look* like? Is it difficult or easy?

It's easy. E-A-S-Y to read. Once through, and you know what you have read! That's what your resume should be.

Magazines, newspapers, and advertising copy are all written in a way (using a special format) that makes them inviting to the eye.

That format is something you already know about: C-O-L-U-M-N-S.

Write your resume in a *column* format! Why? Because it makes the resume easy to scan. And that, my friends, is all that readers want to do with it.

So give them what they want. Give them something easy to read.

▶ How Do You Read, Learn, and Enjoy?

Eye-brain coordination is a miraculous thing. If the eye grabs four, five, six words at a time—in a split second—the brain can put those words in order and make sense of them.

The principle of speed reading says that you can, with your finger as a pacing guide, zoom down the center of a column or a page and let your brain *grab* the words within your eye's field of vision.

The brain then sorts them into the right order almost automatically—as fast as your finger can move down that page!

When your eye must read *across* long lines of type (and especially lines with long words), more concentration is required. Your brain has to think about the meaning of long, unfamiliar words. And eye fatigue results from eye travel across long lines.

How the Eye Reads Down a Page

In English and other Western languages, we read from left to right, starting at the upper-left corner of each page...at the beginning.

Although our eye movement is across and then down each line on an entire page, the *general* "flow" is **diagonal,** from the upper-left corner to the lower-right corner of each page, where the last words on the page are normally found.

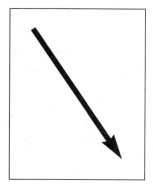

Advertising people call the lower-right corner "the action corner." This is where they place a coupon, a store name, a phone number, or anything they hope will urge you to "act."

The flow, or look, of your resume should guide the reader's eye in the same way that he or she normally reads. The reader's eyes should move down the page from the upper-left corner (where your name and address should appear) to the lower-right corner, where your last words on the page probably appear.

How the Eye Travels Across Lines on a Page

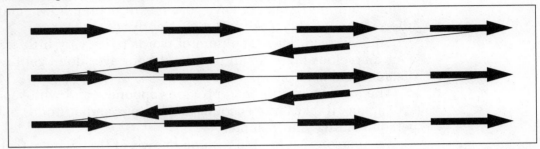

Note that the eye travels along the words in one line. Then, it must travel back across the page, right to left, and seek out the beginning of the next line.

As the eye travels first in one direction, then in the other, and then forward again, it travels *twice the distance* you might, at first, think that it does.

The eye tires quickly. So when you look at a book to see if you might want to purchase it, a book with "all words and very little space" looks difficult to read.

The same is true of a resume. If it contains little white space, and if it is too crowded (especially with long words), the reader gets a very negative first impression!

How the Eye Reads Down a Column

You can either read the way most people do—back and forth, back and forth—or you can read a *better way:*

where	_____
your	
eye	_____
flows	_____
naturally	_____
downward	_____
when	_____
a	_____
column	_____
is	_____
narrow.	_____
▼	_____
▼	_____

When you arrange your resume's body copy in a narrow column, say, 50-55 percent of the width of the page (A column of words that wide would be about 4 to 5 inches in width on a normal 8½ x 11 sheet of paper), you *dramatically* increase the chances that your resume will be *read,* because you have made it *much easier* to read!

In fact, you have made your resume **scannable in 10-20 seconds** merely by improving its readability!

C O N G R A T U L A T I O N S !

Because the rest of the resume writers in the world—hundreds of thousands, even millions—don't know this yet, **you have learned the valued secret of "how to get your resume *read.*"**

In a column format, the eye goes *one* direction: *down;* and it scans all the information quickly, easily, and efficiently.

You can read *down* a column of words (with very little traveling) and let your marvelous brain do all the work! Your eyes don't get tired going all that distance and back again.

The *marketing approach* provides openness and white space to prevent eye fatigue. It takes into account the feelings and attitudes of the *market*—the person reading your resume.

The person reading the resume knows, at first glance, that this will be *easy to read.*

Even if the employer is going through a group of resumes *very quickly,* the ones that look easiest to read are likely to be given preference.

►Use Columns for Eye Appeal

When using a column format, use only *one* column, not two. Any width is acceptable as long as it is easy to read. I prefer narrow columns—ones not exceeding about 50-60 percent of a page width (about 4-5 inches on a normal page).

Think that "less is better." Keep your resume clean looking, with plenty of white space if at all possible.

The reader of your resume may not have the faintest idea about what makes his or her eyes tired, or what makes a page readable. A resume that is easy to read sends the message that "This job seeker is making my job easier."

Their eyes do tell them what they (the eyes) *like* to read and what they *don't like* to read.

Keep this in mind when designing the final draft of your resume. And use *columns* to present your information. Columns *immediately* convey a message.

What message?

"You want to read *this resume* because *this one* is *easy on the eyes.*"

Now, see for yourself, in the following comparison, which format looks more interesting and inviting to you at a casual first glance:

(Set in 2⅜-inch width)

Here is an example of a readable typeface, set in narrow width, for easy readability and quick scanning. If we would set this identical paragraph in a wider format, the eye would have to travel a greater distance to cover the same material, resulting in a tired feeling. Because we learn to read at an early age, and continue to read on through our lifetime, we learn to judge quickly which paragraphs and which kinds of reading look as though they will tire us, and which kinds of reading look inviting and easy to read. Another way to improve readability is to leave the right edge of column-copy rough, or jagged, so that spaces between words are not excessive. If too much space is used, the result is a look of jerkiness rather than smoothness. Words that belong together, such as "Three Blind Mice," should always be placed on the same line, rather than separated on different lines. Also, use hyphens as little as possible; they add jerkiness.

Now, see how much READABILITY the passage loses when it is set in a wider, 6½-inch format:

Here is an example of a readable typeface, set in narrow width, for easy readability and quick scanning. If we would set this identical paragraph in a wider format, the eye would have to travel a greater distance to cover the same material, resulting in a tired feeling. Because we learn to read at an early age, and continue to read on through our lifetime, we learn to judge quickly which paragraphs and which kinds of reading look as though they will tire us, and which kinds of reading look inviting and easy to read. Another way to improve readability is to leave the right edge of column-copy rough, or jagged, so that spaces between words are not excessive. If too much space is used, the result is a look of jerkiness rather than smoothness. Words that belong together, such as "Three Blind Mice," should always be placed on the same line, rather than separated on different lines. Also, use hyphens as little as possible; they add jerkiness.

▶Be Your Own Art Director

In the advertising world, art directors are paid to *design* the page—to put each element, each bit of information, in its proper location:

- So that you read the ad.
- To ensure that you read the important things first as you scan the page.
- To arouse your interest so that you will continue reading.
- And, finally, to get you to *act* on the information you have been given.

So, put yourself in the place of an art director.

You have the challenge of turning a blank piece of paper into an effective promotion piece…something that won't be thrown out or avoided. The message should leap out of your resume at first glance. How?

Use plenty of white space.

Don't crowd your material, giving the reader the impression that your resume is hard to read. It is easier just to toss your resume into the *reject pile!*

Use *design strategy* in planning your resume.

All of us learned to read from upper left to lower right. That's the way our eye naturally glides through any page.

Your resume should be designed, then, so that the eye moves down the page from the upper-left corner down to the lower-right corner.

Underlining is helpful—it breaks up the monotony of a page.

Perhaps, for example, you would like to underline *just* the names of your category headings, such as <u>WORK EXPERIENCE</u>…or the names of the companies/organizations for which you have worked.

Underlining aids readability, but be *consistent* throughout your resume.

Don't change margins in your resume more than necessary.

Changing margins will give your resume a *jerky* look. The look you want to achieve is *smooooooth*. Not jerky.

An exception, however, is a group of words that belong together. If you must go to a second line with a group of words, indent the second line a few spaces. This shows that these words belong with the first line.

Like this:

> *International Farm Machinery and Combine Corporation,*
> *Marketing and Distribution Division*

When describing your school or another *long* proper name, try to keep it on one line.

Do this:

> *Waukesha County Technical College*
> *Pewaukee, Wisconsin*

instead of this:

> *Waukesha County Technical*
> *College*
> *Pewaukee, Wisconsin*

If you *must* separate some of the words in a title, *indent* the word left hanging by itself on the second line. This makes for easier understanding and leaves no question in the reader's mind about which words belong together.

Of course, for every rule there is an exception. And this rule is no exception!

After once listing the full name of an exceptionally long-named school or organization, such as The Mid-State Baptist Institute for Biblical and Theological Studies, it is permissible (and preferable) to abbreviate such a name. But be sensible.

Use "Mid-State Institute" (Not MSBIBTS) because the former is easier for the reader to understand and absorb quickly. So when you write about being on that school's debate team, you could say

Member, championship debate team,
Mid-State Institute, 1981-82

so long as you have previously given the full, more formal, name of the institution in your resume.

Bullets are an excellent way to itemize.

Bullets are *indicators* that tell your eye to "start reading here." They can be written on your typewriter as periods. Or they can be small typewriter o's that you blacken with a fine-point pen.

They call attention to the item and tell the eye, "Start here, eye. This is where you begin to read."

They also tell the reader that this line is going to be short and sweet. Not a long paragraph, but a few short items, with each one preceded by a bullet.

You should separate bullets from the words by two or three spaces. Ad people have used this trick for ages. They still do.

You now know most of what you need to actually write and format a superior resume. The next chapter provides you with tips on how to "package" the resume.

Chapter 5
Packaging & Delivering Your Resume

Get Your Resume Noticed

If you could look through a pile of resumes on any employer's desk, what would you discover?

You'd find (even without reading a single word on a single resume) that most resumes have no *class*.

They're on cheap white paper.

Or they're handwritten.

Or they're done on an ordinary typewriter.

Or they're badly reproduced.

Do you want to be ordinary? To be a carbon copy? Of course not!

Again, put yourself in the reader's place. Think about all those other resumes, and convince yourself that yours has to be *so classy* that it will be *number one* in any stack of also-rans.

You can't see your competition—can't tell whom you are up against—but you know that *you* have to be *number one. Number two loses* when there's only one job!

When you have worked through to the final draft of your resume (carefully worded, edited, shortened, and containing action verbs, results, and accomplishments), you have to consider your resume's final form.

▶ Reproducing Your Resume

Now that you have your resume in its final (and *perfect*) form, you are ready to have it reproduced.

Usually, you will want to have a quantity of resumes, not just one or two. Even if you have prepared your resume for one specific use or person or organization, you may want to keep extras for your personal file. Or, you may need another copy before your resume has become outdated.

The cost of reproducing your resume will vary according to the method you select, where you live, and how many copies you desire.

In most cases, you will prepare a final draft or a *camera-ready* copy, from which any quantity may be reproduced.

If you have access to a computer, a word processor, or an electronic typewriter with memory, you may be able to keep your entire resume *on disk* or in other storage media for later use whenever you need a copy.

But most people will need to prepare the final *perfect* copy and have it reproduced in a quantity reasonable for near-term use. For the average job hunter, this would be 50 to 500 copies.

No matter which method you choose to reproduce your resume, you will need to prepare a final, error-free, fully-proofread *Master Copy* for reproduction.

You now need to select two things: the type style, also called the *typeface* or *font* you prefer, and the method you will use to produce your final copy.

Typefaces

Thousands of different typefaces exist throughout the world. Unless you are associated with the graphic arts or advertising industries, you may not have noticed the differences among them.

For our purposes, I will divide them into just two groups: *serif* and *sans serif* typefaces.

Each typeface, of course, usually contains both uppercase (capital) and lowercase (small) letters. *Serif* typefaces have two important features that *sans serif* typefaces do not:

- Small *appendages,* or "decorative doodads" on the end, top, or bottom of each letter.
- Different *thicknesses,* as you can see in the example shown here. Each letter is both thick and thin, in different places. Here is an example of a serif typeface:

> Prepared, wrote, and managed distribution of all press releases for four Mobil divisions in Chicago region. Supervised two part-time

This combination of thick, then thin, makes letters that are *easier to read,* easier to scan quickly, and easier on the eyes than sans serif typefaces.

Sans serif typefaces, which may appear to be cleaner or less cluttered, are *much* more difficult to read. The following example is identical to the one above except for the typeface.

Prepared, wrote, and managed distribution of all press releases for
four Mobil divisions in Chicago region. Supervised two part-time

Never mix typefaces.

Mixing typefaces gives your resume a cluttered appearance and makes it more difficult to read.

Your resume will look as though you are writing a letter demanding ransom. That is not the effect you want to have.

Sample Typefaces

The following identical lines of type are printed in various serif and sans serif typefaces, in an easy-to-read column format. Compare for yourself and see which you prefer for readability.

TYPEFACE GUIDELINES

Possible Typeface	Good Choice Yes/No
Avant Garde Prepared, wrote, and managed distribution of all press releases for four Mobil divisions in Chicago region. Supervised two part-time	No Sans serif
Helvetica Prepared, wrote, and managed distribution of all press releases for four Mobil divisions in Chicago region. Supervised two part-time	No Sans serif
Helvetica Condensed Prepared, wrote, and managed distribution of all press releases for four Mobil divisions in Chicago region. Supervised two part-time	No Sans serif, unattractive, and ordinary
ITC Bookman Prepared, wrote, and managed distribution of all press releases for four Mobil divisions in Chicago region. Supervised two part-time	Yes Serif
Times Prepared, wrote, and managed distribution of all press releases for four Mobil divisions in Chicago region. Supervised two part-time	Yes Serif
Times Bold **Prepared, wrote, and managed distribution of all press releases for four Mobil divisions in Chicago region. Supervised two part-time**	No Serif, too heavy for resume body use, for high-lighting and headings

TYPEFACE GUIDELINES

Possible Typeface	Good Choice Yes/No
New Century Schoolbook	**Yes**
Prepared, wrote, and managed distribution of all press releases for four Mobil divisions in Chicago region. Supervised two part-time	Serif
Palatino	**Yes**
Prepared, wrote, and managed distribution of all press releases for four Mobil divisions in Chicago region. Supervised two part-time	Serif
ITC Zaph Chancery	**No**
Prepared, wrote, and managed distribution of all press releases for four Mobil divisions in Chicago region. Supervised two part-time	Serif, too gaudy, not businesslike

►Make Your Resume First Class

Your final copy must be typed on a top-quality sheet of *bright white* paper. It should be a paper on which the black typeface shows up well, with good contrast between black and white.

If for your final resume copy you use a typewriter, it should be an office-quality machine—one that uses a carbon ribbon cartridge.

Old-fashioned typewriters (such as the ones many of us have in our homes) use felt or fabric ribbons. These ribbons have the advantage of lasting for months or even years, but with each succeeding winding or use, the ribbon loses some degree of intensity. After you have used it many times, the contrast has diminished to poor.

Newer machines use cartridge ribbons, almost all of which are carbon ribbons or film ribbons. The older types are thick; the newer ones are thin, much like the tape in an audio or video cassette. They are wound onto a spool and then packed in a cartridge that slips easily onto your electronic typewriter or computer spindle.

Each impression made by a carbon ribbon cartridge is clean and crisp, with excellent contrast between the black letters and the white paper. Perhaps you are one of the lucky people who have access to a word processor, personal computer, or a large mainframe computer.

But what counts is that you must have a letter-quality printer. If it is a daisywheel or similar printer, it must have a carbon ribbon cartridge.

A "near letter quality" or a dot-matrix printer is *not* acceptable.

Laser and inkjet printers, of course, are usually excellent. Generally, laser printers also provide proportional-spacing typefaces. These allocate more space for the letter "M," for instance, than they would for the letter "I" because the "M" is much wider.

Non-proportional-spacing machines give an "I" the same amount of space as an "M," and this detracts from the readability and appearance of the words.

Computer-Generated and Typeset Resumes

Resumes done according to a "formula" are sometimes frowned on by personnel professionals.

If a resume looks as if it has been prepared according to a formula, it may appear that the sender is interested in *any* job, not necessarily in the reader's specific job.

Typeset resumes have also been looked upon with skepticism by some "experts." Typeset resumes were thought to be "too slick," probably mass-produced, and possibly the work of a professional resume writer, rather than the writer's own work.

What do the experts suggest?

Have your resume on a computer diskette or stored in your electronic typewriter.

Then print an original each time. That way, the ribbon density, type appearance, etc., will match your cover letter (individually typed at about the same time, we assume). This will create the impression that "I did this resume just for you because I'm interested in the job you have available...not just any job."

An added benefit: you can modify various versions easily to emphasize or de-emphasize something, to tailor the Job Objective to the position available, etc. It's more trouble for you, but it makes a much better impression than do mass-produced resumes.

Whatever method you use, do your final perfect copy on bright white paper. Then you are ready to have it reproduced in quantity. Or you can store it in memory for future additional copies.

In the twenty-five years I have been reading, reviewing, and evaluating resumes, I have seen all sizes, shapes, formats, colors, typefaces, and methods of reproduction.

Even though it may seem like overkill, check the following lists to see which methods of reproduction are *acceptable,* which ones *may be acceptable,* and which are *not acceptable,* when you are making your choices.

Acceptable Means of Reproducing Your Resume

- Offset Printing (as found at the many commercial print shops that will produce quick and economical copies for you)
- Office-quality (floor-model) photocopy machine
- Letter-quality printer with cartridge ribbon
- Computer laser printer using serif typefaces
- Office-quality electronic typewriter, serif typeface
- Office-quality electric typewriter, serif typeface

Nonacceptable Methods of Reproducing Your Resume

- Hand-written or hand-lettered
- Stencil process
- Mimeograph machine
- Fabric ribbon typewriter
- Home-quality portable typewriter, fabric or ribbon cartridge
- Script (simulated handwriting) typewriter of any quality
- Ditto process

- All-capital-letters typewriter of any quality
- Dot-matrix computer printer, 9-pin, 24-pin, etc.
- Near-letter-quality computer printer, any quality
- Copy machine that produces anything less than excellent quality copies

"Maybe" Acceptable Methods of Reproducing Your Resume

- Table-model photocopy machine (using plain paper)
- Professional typesetting by printer or typesetter
- Old-style office-quality typewriter with metal characters and featuring variable or proportional spacing

▶ Evaluating Your Print Shop

Choose your print shop carefully. You will find considerable differences in price and quality among printers.

Ask friends for recommendations of printers. Then call or visit several to compare prices, available paper stocks, colors, weights, finishes, and quality.

Ask printers to show you samples of their work. Ask if there is an extra charge for making a plate if you plan to have your resumes printed by the offset process.

If the print shop uses a photocopy machine for most resumes, make sure it makes good quality copies before your resumes are reproduced on it.

Be absolutely sure that your resume is *exactly* the way you want it when you give it to the printer. It is *your* responsibility, not the printer's, if you discover a mistake after the printer has printed 50, 100, or 500 resumes!

You might be surprised to learn how many people discover mistakes *after* paying for the resume, only to have to pay *again* after the mistakes have been noticed and corrected.

If the printer offers to prepare the final copy of your resume and you decide to have the printer do it, or if you turn this task over to someone other than yourself—or to someone you can watch or supervise—tell that person *not to change* **anything.**

Not a word. Not a space. Not a line.

Don't allow the person even to move a word to another line. Not **anything.**

You are paying, or trusting, that person to *type* what you have prepared, and to do so exactly as you want it done.

You are the boss. And *you* have read this book. They have not. You know more about what you want than your typist does.

You are probably right. And *that person* is probably wrong.

And be sure to proofread the new version. Mistakes often creep in, and you'll want to find them now before the resume is printed.

▶ Selecting the Paper Stock for Your Resume

Color

The best color for your resume is probably a slightly off-white, eggshell color, sometimes called ecru. The next-best color would be a classy, elegant white.

Beyond these, you might consider ivory, but not one that is too yellow. You can also use a *very* light tan or buff.

Other colors are risky. Because they may offend the reader who does not like the particular color you have selected.

What about gray? You may love it; I do. But gray, even light gray, can also look like dirty white. And black ink on dark gray, which is one of my favorite colors, is difficult to read.

All dark color papers, of course, are difficult to read. I have seen resumes printed on dark brown paper with black ink. They were difficult, almost impossible, to read.

So was a resume printed on brilliant purple, with *white ink*. The applicant, no doubt, thought that he was going to be different. But being different is not always a positive trait. This time, it got the candidate laughed at, not admired.

Yes, a brilliant color certainly would stand out in a stack of white resumes. But just as a brilliantly colored chartreuse home might lower property values in a neighborhood, a garish resume would almost certainly lower your value as a candidate for employment.

I know one young man who used a brilliant yellow paper, with his name boldly printed across the top in dark brown ink. It was indeed memorable.

It resembled a breakfast menu at a fast-food restaurant. And normally, it would be considered in poor taste.

But he was sending it to advertising agencies—the larger ones that receive thousands of ordinary resumes. This one stood out. And it got the candidate in.

He was granted an interview. And he got the job. (What's more, he is still there, some fifteen years later.)

But not everyone is applying to advertising agencies. So choose your color *carefully* and with an eye toward who will be reading your resume.

Texture and Weight

Paper also has *texture* differences. Linen, pebble finish, vellum, gloss, enamel, and laid finish are just a few of the many textures available.

Choose the one you like best, but consider also the person and organization you're sending it to.

For most resumes, you should select a finish that has an executive look and feel, rather than something that appeals to the emotions or to your sensual nature.

Paper also has various weights. You've noticed that some papers are very light, such as overseas airmail stationery. And that some papers are very heavy, almost like cardboard.

For the business resume, a medium weight is usually appropriate. If the printer gives you a choice between two weights, it is usually better to select the slightly heavier stock, even if it costs more.

When you receive a wedding invitation that immediately feels like a high quality paper, you get a very favorable impression even before you open the envelope.

You should strive to create the same impression when someone first handles your resume. And you can do this by choosing your paper stock carefully.

The finest grades of paper are made of 100 percent cotton fiber or 100 percent rag content. Most cheap papers are made of 100 percent wood pulp.

Some very fine papers are made from 75 percent wood pulp and 25 percent fiber. In the trade, printers refer to this as "25 percent rag" paper. It is quite acceptable for resumes.

▶ Final Touches

What about colored ink?

It costs considerably more to have a special ink color for your resume. Printers normally use black ink. And every time they print in a color other than black, they must stop, clean the press completely, and change the ink—just for you.

You must pay for mixing the extra ink color especially for you, and for the time and labor required to clean and change the press. The cost for this might be as much as it costs to print your resumes in the first place.

Black ink is not only acceptable but preferred for most business situations. The minimum number of printed copies you should get is 100.

You may need only a few now, but the cost is slight for an extra 50 or so. Get estimates from the printer on the cost for 100 copies and for even more copies if you think you might use them.

Then opt for a number that will carry you through the next few weeks or months without having to have more printed.

▶ Stationery and Envelopes

Stationery, which you'll need for your cover letters, can be expensive.

I recommend, in keeping with your desire to convey a good image, that you type your cover letters on good quality paper—like your resume.

Instead of going to the stationery store and paying for paper in a fancy box, ask the printer if you may purchase some stationery in bulk—the same high-quality paper on which your resume is being printed.

The printer may just throw it in at no extra charge because he or she is in the printing business, not the paper business. (Printers buy their paper at wholesale prices.) Ask.

You may want to try to get matching business-size envelopes too. But standard white business envelopes will do nicely in most situations.

You can buy a package of decent enough envelopes almost anywhere for a dollar or two. The printer may also have envelopes that match the paper you selected, so it is worth asking.

Some stationery stores also carry good-quality writing paper in bulk, with matching envelopes. You can buy it by the pound or by the sheet. If your city is large enough to have stores that specialize in good writing papers, a phone call or two will determine which ones sell good paper in bulk (without the expensive fancy boxes and ribbons).

Now you know about good paper, the right typefaces, and the other "little things" that separate outstanding resumes from those that are merely adequate.

Taken together with the other things you have learned, you have the information to make your resume stand out for all the "right" reasons.

After more than 15 years of research and testing, I know these techniques work. Most people "strongly" prefer the resume format I have developed and now recommend to you.

Many of them are experienced executives...men and women who have seen thousands of resumes.

Even *they* often don't know exactly *why* they like this format. But like it, and prefer it, they do!

Chapter 6
Sample Resumes & Worksheets

Choose a Style That Fits

It's now time to actually create your resume. And you are ready to do just that.

Look over the sample resumes in the first part of this chapter. They are all based on what I have seen in *real* resumes. The names, addresses, and other details have been changed, of course.

Some of the sample resumes break some of the "rules" but are included anyway. There is, after all, no "perfect" resume. Nor is there just one way to write one. Each person is different, and each resume will, likewise, have its own personality.

For each sample resume, I have written notes about the person behind the resume. This will help you understand why that resume was done in the way it was done.

And since some of the resumes have "flaws" of various kinds (or at least things that might have been done differently), I have added notes about these—as well as the things I liked.

I hope this approach helps you. Look over the examples carefully and jot down ideas you want to consider for your own resume.

At the end of the chapter, after all the sample resumes, is a thorough resume worksheet. Complete it carefully, and it (and the rest of the information in this book) will give you all of the information you will need to write your own resume. It is that simple.

When you are done with the worksheet, use the checklist at the end of this chapter to help you avoid common resume mistakes. Pay attention to the various final tips for "writing your resume to get *results*."

►Sample Resumes

MARK M. SCOVILLE
1452 4th Avenue North
St. Cloud, Minnesota 56301
(612) 555-8201

Permanent Address:
31 Overlook Road
Blue Sky, Minnesota 55352
(612) 555-3574

Job Objective: Entry-Level Financial Analyst
with Portfolio Management or Financial Organization

EDUCATION

Since he is still a student, education is emphasized by placement above the experience section.

Bachelor of Science degree in Business Administration
St. Cloud State University, St. Cloud, Minnesota
Major: Finance; Minor: Economics
Date of Graduation: November, 1994
Grade Average: 3.146/4.0

WORK EXPERIENCE

October, 1992
to
Present

Park National Bank
St. Cloud, Minnesota

Computer Operator

Work nights; update daily files, process reports, back up complete computer system, print notices, sort checks on reader sorter.

March, 1991
to
September, 1991

Able Charlie Manufacturing Corporation
Bloomington, Minnesota

Project Worker

Processed insurance claims in excess of $1,000,000. Used Lotus 1-2-3 and dBASE III extensively.

March, 1990
to
December, 1990

Topper Automotive of Minnesota, Inc.
Goldenrod, Minnesota

Data Processing

Responsible for updating files, inventory control, processing of reports, some data entry. Received training at corporate office in Kansas City, Kansas.

ACTIVITIES & INTERESTS

- Selected for President's Round Table (all-university plan board)
- Vice-President, Delta Sigma Pi (business fraternity)
- President, Financial Management Association, SCSU
- Advisor, Junior Achievement; voted "Company of the Year"
- Selected and secured national speaker for Career Days
- Hobbies: sports, camping, fishing, music

Linda G. Marsala-Winston

6673 East Avenue
Lakeland, California 94544
(415) 555-1519
(415) 555-6755 (leave message)

Career Objective: Copywriter, Account Executive in
Advertising or Public Relations Agency

Experience

- **COPYWRITER.** Developed copy for direct mail catalogues featuring collectible items, for real estate developments and for agricultural machinery and equipment.

- **WRITER.** Wrote for *Habitat* magazine in London, England. Specialized in Architecture, Contemporary Lifestyles, and Interior Design.

- **SALES PROMOTION.** Fullmer's Department Store, Honolulu, Hawaii. Developed theme and copy for 1981 Grand Opening of Far East Department.

- **FABRIC DESIGNER.** Award-winning textile designer and importer of African and South American textiles.

- **OTHER WRITING AND PROMOTION.** News bureau chief and feature writer for college newspaper. Contributor to literary magazine. College Board Representative, *Mademoiselle* magazine. Scrip writer for fashion shows. Won creative writing fellowship for study in Mexico. Did public relations for International Cotton Conference. Summer graduate fellow in public information, United Nations, New York City.

- **TEACHER.** Instructor in professional studies department of London Career Training Institute. In charge of group dynamics and career guidance module. Organized a team for "Women in Development."

Education

- Bachelor of Arts degree in English, University of California, Berkeley

- Graduate study, 30 credits completed in Journalism, University of California, Berkeley

- Master of Arts Degree in Guidance and Counseling, California State University, Fresno

Membership

- Member, San Francisco Women in Advertising

Jean Mary Gendlin
3939 South Fortune Circle
Reading, Pennsylvania 19600
(215) 555-0562
(215) 555-6703 (message)

Job Objective: Clerk in Retail Soft Goods or Women's Wear Store
(part-time: afternoons and weekends)

EDUCATION

Reading Wilson High School
Graduation: May, 19XX
College Preparatory Program
3.21/4.0 Grade Point Average

SCHOOL ACTIVITIES AND HONORS

- Vice-President, Future Business Leaders of America, 1994-95, Reading Wilson Chapter

- Selected to work as Attendance Clerk in School Office, junior year

- Selected to sing in Chamber Choir (one of 16 students)

- Active in girls' athletics, intramural sports activities

- Member, Home Economics Club, 2 years

EXTRACURRICULAR ORGANIZATIONS

- Secretary, church youth group; write all minutes, keep attendance records for funding purposes

- Honored Princess, Bethel #14, Order of Job's Daughters

WORK EXPERIENCE

- Baby-sitter since age 11 for neighborhood families

- Summers: Counselor for girls ages 6-9, at YWCA Day Camp for Disabled Children, 1993, 1994

REFERENCES

- References will be furnished on request from employers, teachers, pastor, and others.

Brian Scott Molitor
1045 Applewood Lane
Cupertino, California 95015
(213) 422-0864
(213) 555-6642 (alternative phone)

Job Objective: Auto Mechanic

EDUCATION

San Diablo Community College
Mount Carmel, California
Certificate in Auto Mechanics; 3.25/4.0 grade average
2-year Certificate in Auto Mechanics, awarded May, 1994

Mount Carmel High School
Mount Carmel, California
Date of Graduation: June, 1992

WORK EXPERIENCE

June, 1991
to
Present

Charlie Moss Mobil Service
Mount Carmel, California

Assistant Manager/Mechanic

• Qualified in virtually all kinds of mechanical and electronic repairs on domestic and foreign cars:

  • Electronic tune-ups
  • Computer command control systems
  • Front-end work and alignment
  • Transaxle work
  • Transmission diagnosis and repair
  • Complete engine overhaul

• Hired as high school student for summer and part-time work, later given responsibility to close and lock station, make bank deposits; promoted to assistant manager for weekend shifts. Supervised four employees.

June, 1990
to
May, 1991

Hunter's Pharmacy
Mount Carmel, California

Retail Sales Clerk

• Waited on customers at full-service pharmacy. Stocked and inventoried products. Made deliveries to customers. Drove van. Worked part-time afternoons and weekends.

<u>SCHOOL AND COMMUNITY ACTIVITIES</u>

- Elected Vice-President, college VICA Club, 1992-93

- Won regional and state 1st-place awards in VICA competitions, 1992, 1993 (Auto Mechanics Division)

- Active in intramural sports throughout high school

- Participated in Community Clean-up: spring, 1990 and 1991

- Played solo in annual band concert (trumpet), 1990

<u>PERSONAL INFORMATION</u>

> Mentioning age, height, and weight are not necessary but can be included if information will help in some way.

- Born May 13, 1970; excellent health

- Height: 5 feet, 10 inches; weight, 165 pounds

- Have overhauled four auto engines; have worked on cars as a hobby since age 13

- Other interests: all sports, fixing anything, camping

<u>REFERENCES</u>

"Brian is dependable and friendly. Our customers like him, and we have been pleased with his work. I would be happy if my own sons turn out like Brian."

> Charlie Moss, owner
> Charlie Moss Mobile Service

"Brian has been a leader in VICA and an excellent student in our Auto Mechanics program. He's not afraid of hard work, staying late, or learning new technologies. I recommend him very highly."

> William Meier, Instructor
> San Diablo Community College

- Additional personal and business references are available and will be furnished on request.

Andrea M. Salter
1200 Mall Avenue
State College, Pennsylvania 21101
(215) 555-6239
(215) 555-7732 (messages)

CAREER OBJECTIVE
Director of Audiovisual Instructional Media

EMPLOYMENT HISTORY

August, 1992
to
Present

Pennsylvania State University
State College, Pennsylvania

Head, Department of Instructional Media
Supervise 15 employees, plus 40 students as part-time staff. Propose and control budget. Administer complete department, including microforms, films, videotapes, transparencies. Provide all media services to campus:

- Graphic arts and photography
- Circulation of audiovisual equipment
- Operator assistance and scheduling
- Production of slide programs
- Production of videotapes
- Minor repairs, troubleshooting, and general maintenance
- Consultation on creative production topics to faculty and staff

Recommend and purchase hardware, software, supplies, rentals. Approve all services and procedures. Recommend and supervise design, construction, and scheduling of all facilities.

Develop, implement, and supervise all policies and guidelines for instructional media, including security and inventory control.

January, 1989
to
August, 1992

Kimball Broadcasting Corporation/KKBC
Las Vegas, Nevada

Assistant Engineer for Audio
Designed, updated, and upgraded complete radio broadcasting facility and studio. Contracted for and supervised erecting of tower. Recommended equipment; purchased complete studio. Installed and repaired equipment.

EMPLOYMENT HISTORY (continued)

Kimball Broadcasting Corporation/KKBC
Wrote operating policies and guidelines. Ensured compliance with FCC regulations. Recommended programming policies and changes to improve ratings. Handled all on-location broadcasts. Worked with on-air personalities. Trained employees.

EDUCATION

Master of Science degree in Media, 1989
University of Wisconsin - Stout
Grade average: 3.85/4.0

Bachelor of Arts degree in Business Administration
University of Southern Iowa, 1987
Rolland, Iowa

Information gives impression job seeker gets involved and will succeed in her profession.

PROFESSIONAL AFFILIATIONS

- Information in *Who's Who in American Colleges and Universities*, 1986-1987.

- Instructor in Media Techniques, University of Southern Iowa

- Member, Business and Professional Media People

REFERENCES

- Business, personal, and educational references are available and will be furnished on request

Conor R. O'Brien
14567 Treeful Lane
Walnut Springs, New Jersey 01111
(202) 555-6421
(202) 555-6602 (leave message)

Successfully used combination resume to escape disagreeable boss and get into sales side of computer industry. Background in field service and management are strong points for selling systems into similar environments.

OBJECTIVE: to be a hands-on, accomplished MANAGER
selling and providing high-quality technical services
in the computer hardware or software industry

SUMMARY OF EXPERIENCES

This summary is extra, not necessary, but is nice touch.

- Plant Manager: 100% responsible for production of state-of-the-art advanced electronics equipment
- Planner and Achiever: Analyzing situations to achieve specific goals and results
- Financial Manager: Manage complex projects with budgetary concerns in mind

ACHIEVEMENTS

- Promoted to Leading Support Technician in charge of Englander Electronics' Rohrer System
- Successfully dealt with customers, salesmen, and field service technicians, using honesty, diplomacy, and confidence; provided superior technical support
- Personally evaluated and selected all test equipment used in manufacturing end-product (over $100,000 worth of equipment)
- Directly responsible for expanding and maintaining manufacturing workforce that grew over 500% in 3 years (began with one person, grew to 20 people)

EXPERIENCE

Deather Instrument Company, Earthworm, New Jersey
Production Manager, 1990 to present
Manufacturer of state-of-the-art electrocardiograph equipment

- Responsible for overseeing manufacturing of medical electronics from prototype to finished product (1988 sales: $10,000,000)

Englander Electronics, Mollica, New Jersey
Field Service Engineer, 1985 to 1990
Manufacturer of electrocardiographs and intensive care monitors

- Hired as production technician; promoted through system to Tech Support Engineer to top position as Field Service Engineer

Buzzell Controls Manufacturing Company, Loveland, New Jersey
Manufacturing Consultant, 1983 to 1985
Manufacturer of high-grade industrial motor controls

Resume could be forced into one-page format but would look crowded and not be as effective.

PERSONAL INFORMATION

- Honor Student in college; selected for Director's Honors List

- Member, Electronics Club, 1981-82, 1982-83

- Earnings from working in retail sales at Spring Garden Center (3 years) paid 100% of college expenses

- Enjoy playing basketball, scuba diving, swimming, all sports

- Played church league basketball, 2 years; played in 2 summer softball leagues

- Have traveled throughout the United States, including Alaska and Hawaii, on business and for pleasure

- Hobbies: photography, woodworking, home ownership

- Happily married to Lisa O'Brien since 1986; 2 children, ages 3 and 2

EDUCATION

Waltrip County Technical College
Associate Degree in Electronics, 1983

Amy Ann Towson
4848 Sedler Parkway
Billings, Montana 59101
(406) 555-7856

CAREER OBJECTIVE: Secretarial Position in Broadcasting
Requiring Excellent Word Processing Skills and Some Public Contact

EDUCATION

Secretarial Office Skills Institute
Seattle, Washington
Diploma in Secretarial Science
Graduation: June, 1995
Honor Student; 3.5 overall grade average

East High School
Billings, Montana
Graduation: May, 1992
"B+" grade average; elected to Honor Roll

WORK EXPERIENCE

September, 1992
to
Present

Bruce, Carl & Douglas Law Offices
Seattle, Washington

Office Assistant
Typed correspondence, reports, simple briefs, and various forms for attorneys and paralegals. Answered phone, took messages, and acted as fill-in receptionist. Part-time job while attending Secretarial Office Skills Institute.

Skills levels: type 70 words per minute, take shorthand at normal conversational speed, operate IBM-compatible personal computer and all normal office equipment (calculator, photocopier, postage meter, mail room machines).

September, 1989
to
May, 1992

East High School
Billings, Montana

Office Assistant
Typed reports and forms, ran errands, processed attendance reports, and answered phone; part-time job during free periods, after school, and on some vacation days.

WORK EXPERIENCE (continued)

Summers, 1991,   <u>All-Hours Convenience Store</u>
1992, 1993   Billings, Montana

<u>Clerk</u>
Sold packaged products, deli items, sandwiches; stocked shelves; took inventory; acted as Assistant Manager during absence of regular managers (given key to store, made bank deposits).

Summers, 1991,   <u>Family Nursing Home</u>
1992, 1993   Billings, Montana

<u>Volunteer Aide</u>
Assisted staff with projects; visited with residents; helped in crafts sessions and sing-alongs. Worked 4-6 hours weekly.

CIVIC AND COMMUNITY ACTIVITIES

> Includes number of points in this section. Details could give an edge.

- Volunteered for "Habitat for Humanity" project; met and worked with ex-President Carter.

- Active on Academy Student Council; helped plan school picnic, field trips, and other student events.

- Secretary, East High School Office Careers Club; elected by classmates.

- Active in church youth group; elected to various offices, including President.

Daniel A. Kohl
3606 Roxboro Road
Atlanta, Georgia 30326-1455
(404) 551-4040

JOB OBJECTIVE: Systems Analyst/Management Information Systems

WORK EXPERIENCE

ACCOMPLISHMENTS

- Exceeded 135% of sales quota, won "leading salesperson award" calling exclusively on new prospects to sell point-of-purchase recordkeeping and cash flow systems for Sweda Division, Litton Industries.

- Qualified programmer, trainer, installer for data processing equipment. Achieved 50% of sales through referral of clients. "Dan was the best sales and service representative we've ever had calling on us," said Allan Koehn, CEO, Circle G. Restaurants.

- Developed complete recordkeeping and accounting system for Georgia's largest cosmetics wholesaler. Trained employees, supervised initial operations, debugged system.

- Increased sales 71% over prior year in Georgia/Florida territory for Chicago-based manufacturer of electric blankets and appliances (Midwest Appliances Corporation).

EDUCATION

- Graduated from University of Illinois, 1981, Marketing/Management major, Bachelor of Science degree.

- Currently enrolled in graduate studies, Georgia State University, Atlanta, leading to M.B.A. degree with computer science emphasis.

- Graduated from Harcourt College, private business college. Awarded 2-year Associate Degree in Business.

- Graduated from NCR School, Computer Programming, 1982.

PERSONAL INFORMATION

- President, college fraternity, Tau Sigma Epsilon

- News editor, University of Illinois Campus Events newspaper

- Enjoy sports, classical music, reading business books

- Member, Buckhead Jaycees; chair, Special Olympics Project (raised $8,000 for fund)

EMPLOYMENT HISTORY

Record of holding jobs not good because of moving around. It is tucked on second page. Could have used skills resume to hide tenure on jobs completely.

- November, 1984, to Present: Territory Sales Representative Sweda Division, Litton Industries Atlanta, Georgia

- November, 1982, to November, 1984: Sales Representative Collins Cosmetics Corporation Atlanta, Georgia

- November, 1981, to October, 1982: District Sales Manager Midwest Appliances Corp., Chicago

- Held various part-time sales jobs during college years to support myself independently; paid all college tuition and expenses

PERSONAL INFORMATION

- Willing to travel if desired; have traveled widely throughout United States, Canada, Mexico

Norman P. Mindell
1042 North Amber Way
Charlotte, North Carolina
(602) 555-8745 (work)
(602) 555-9631 (answering service)

JOB OBJECTIVE:
Automobile Dealership New Car Sales Manager

WORK EXPERIENCE

October, 1990
to
Present

Sanders Chevrolet
Charlotte, North Carolina

Used Car Sales Manager

Sell used cars and manage sales force of four salespeople. Consistently exceed quota by at least 10%, often 25%. Have own clientele; 30% of personal production is from referrals and recommendations. Conduct sales meetings for staff. Hold training sessions; establish sales quotas for dealership. Purchase cars at auctions; travel to various auctions. Awarded trip to Hawaii for performance.

April, 1988
to
October, 1990

Sanders Chevrolet
Charlotte, North Carolina

Sales Representative, Used Cars

Sold used cars. Consistently averaged sales of 25 cars monthly in good months. 15 cars in slow months. Set company record for unit sales and total volume. Promoted to Sales Manager after 2 and 1/2 years over salespeople with more experience and seniority. Started as part-timer while attending college full-time.

PERSONAL INFORMATION

- Graduated from Piedmont Junior College
  Associate Degree in Marketing, Class of 1988

- Honor Roll Student: 3.47 grade average;
  Vice President of Marketing Club

- Have enjoyed cars as a hobby since childhood.
  Mechanically inclined; built kit car at age 20.

- Active in church and civic affairs. Member, Jaycees.
  Host and referee/judge, Special Olympics.

Amy Jo Gibbs
Apartment #206
32 Towne Circle
Philadelphia, Pennsylvania 19177
(215) 555-3911
(215) 555-7675 (for messages)

Career and Job Target: Assistant Buyer for Fashion or Soft Goods

EDUCATION

Fashion Academy of Philadelphia
Associate Degree in Fashion Merchandising
Graduated "With Honors," June, 1994

Toledo Area Community College, Toledo, Ohio
Studied Business and Conversational French

Woodrow Wilson High School, Toledo, Ohio
Graduated May, 1991; B+ average, upper 1/4 of class

WORK EXPERIENCE

- Retail Sales Representative, "The Up Shop"
  Warrington's Department Store, Philadelphia

  Sell business clothing and ensembles for business women in special section of store. Assisted in some buying decisions. Worked 30 hours per week while attending Fashion Academy of Philadelphia. Assigned to supervise training program for two high school co-op students.

- Sales Clerk in Cosmetics, Walgreen's
  Toledo, Ohio (two years)

  Sold cosmetics at counter part-time while in high school. Received school credit under school's Marketing Education co-op program.

COMMUNITY AND SCHOOL ACTIVITIES AND ORGANIZATIONS

- Vice President, Fashionettes Modeling Club (sponsors of annual charity "Fashion Fair" to raise scholarship funds for students and charitable causes)

- Member, Student Senate, Fashion Academy, 2 years

- High school: marching band, sports, various clubs, Honor Roll

John M. Thomas
2248 North 67th Avenue
Phoenix, Arizona 85355
(602) 555-5623 (Home)
(602) 555-1428 (Message)

JOB OBJECTIVE: Advertising Art Director
(Layout, Design, Illustration) . . . in a position
using my communication abilities in working well with others

EXPERIENCE

October, 1987
to
June, 1994

Turnbull, Teller and Witsend Advertising
Phoenix, Arizona

Art Director

- Work with account executives, copywriters, creative director to create and develop initial ideas for clients, often under tight deadlines. Supervise five artists; delegate assignments; work with printers, paper suppliers, typographers.

- Work on Macintosh II Desktop Publisher using PageMaker, Lightspeed, and other software programs.

- Accounts include:
  - Union Batteries • Abbott Seeds
  - Color Factory • Suburban Pools
  - Motel 8 • Hartwell Home Organs
  - Area Chevy Dealers • Med Pharm
  - 1st National Bank • Romer Faucets
  - KinderCare Institute • MillWay Homes

February, 1981
to
October, 1987

Roberson and Michaels Advertising
Scottsdale, Arizona

Art Director

- Layout, keyline/paste-up for local, regional, and national accounts: motels, dry cleaners, hobby shops, auto dealers, shopping malls, national Foodsaver markets chain.

June, 1979
to
February, 1981

Sun Valley Banking Corporation
Phoenix, Arizona

Artist and Designer

- Prepared in-house ads, brochures, mailers, inserts, annual reports, forms.

SPECIAL PROJECTS   Mention of recognizable brand names increases stature as accomplished professional.

- Won National First Place Award for Phoenix Junior Advertising Club as chair of competitive creative team for Y-Pals (YMCA program for fatherless boys), 1986.

- Freelance illustration and design for Hewlett-Packard, Sky Harbor Airport, Arizona Medical Society, McDonald's.

EDUCATION

- Arizona State University
Bachelor of Fine Arts degree in
Visual Communications
Degree granted June, 1979

- Valley High School
Phoenix, Arizona
Graduated with diploma, honors

HOBBIES AND INTERESTS

- Photography, illustration, outdoor sports; family events with wife, Andrea, and three children.

DAVID C. GERMANN
1604 North 105th Street
Nashville, Tennessee 37200
(615) 555-0789 (leave message)

Here's a recent grad, strong on college activities and school leadership but weak on job experience. He correctly leads off with his best stuff first, his leadership activities. "Tell 'em what sells 'em."

CAREER OBJECTIVE
Teaching Position in Junior High or Middle School
in Social Studies, Geography, or Government

EDUCATION

Tennessee College, Nashville, Tennessee
Bachelor of Arts, May, 1994
Major: Education; Minor: Social Studies and Geography
Grade Average: 3.7 on 4.0 System

Johnson City High School, Johnson City, Tennessee
Graduated June, 1990
Ranked 28th in class of 415

HONORS, AWARDS, AND ACHIEVEMENTS

(He had even more activities than these, but he wisely pared them down to only the more important ones.)

- Dean's List, Tennessee College (3.5 required)

- Selected for listing and membership (junior year) in *Who's Who in American Colleges and Universities*

- Winner, Scroll Award for Academic and Service Leadership

- President, Kappa Delta Pi, National Education Honor Society, (Tennessee College Chapter)

- Treasurer, Phi Eta Sigma, National Freshman Honor Society (Tennessee College Chapter)

- Cochair, Campus Chest, 1992, 1993; raised $8,000 for Emergency Student Loan Fund

- Selected for membership, Tennessee College Activities Board, junior and senior years

- Selected for Winterim Social Planning Board

Note that his high school years are given less importance/space.

- High School: elected to National Honor Society in junior year; member and officer of numerous clubs and organizations; teacher's aide (for kindergarten) for one semester

WORK EXPERIENCE

His job experience is not impressive, so it's barely more than mentioned.

Remember: If you're 55 years old, write little or nothing about what you did thirty years ago.

- September, 1993 to May, 1994
  Tennessee College, Nashville, Tennessee
  Activities Program Facilitator

  Planned programming for residence hall activities. Acted as liaison between Resident Assistants and Administration. Published residence hall newsletter. Gained experience in advising, counseling, and referral of students for professional counseling.

WORK EXPERIENCE (continued)

- September, 1992, to December, 1993
  Tennessee College
  Geography Lab Assistant

  Aided students in audiovisual tutorial laboratory.

- September, 1991, to May, 1992
  Tennessee College
  Dormitory Switchboard Operator

- Summers, 1990 through 1993
  Summer painting and maintenance for various employers in
  Johnson City, Tennessee (customer names furnished on request)

PERSONAL INFORMATION

- President, United Christian Youth Organizations (consortium of all
  Johnson City church youth groups); active member, church youth
  group; president, senior year

- Play piano, string bass, guitar

- Enjoy athletics and all sports, growing greenhouse plants, travel

- Through scholarships and personal earnings, earned funds to pay
  80% of college expenses

REFERENCES

- School, business, and personal references are available and will
  gladly be furnished on request.

Note: Dave Germann writes "earned funds to pay 80%." That's a great way to indicate your college work history, and the fact that you paid a substantial portion of your college expenses, instead of being given money on a silver platter. It's better to write it this way than to add uninteresting details about restaurants you worked at, where you waited tables, stores you clerked in, etc.

If you worked a series of short-term or temporary jobs, you shouldn't list them all. Instead, group them and say something like what Dave said: that you worked various jobs and paid a percentage of school expenses, or that you "held several part-time jobs in college."

KAREN E. MULLIGAN
669 Dart Drive
Marietta, Georgia 30033
(404) 555-1571
(404) 555-4534 (alternative phone)

EDUCATION

Emory University School of Law
Atlanta, Georgia
Class of 19XX

University of Alabama, Huntsville
Graduated February, 1992, with high honors: "Magna cum Laude"
Bachelor of Arts degree; Major, psychology; minor, political science

Decatur High School, Decatur, Alabama
Class of 1987

HONORS, AWARDS, AND ACHIEVEMENTS

- Selected "Outstanding Graduate," Department of Psychology, University of Alabama, Huntsville, 1992

- Elected to Pi Sigma Alpha, political science honor society

- Elected to Alpha Lambda Delta, freshman honor society

- Selected for all-university Concert Committee: worked for four years to help select concerts for campus and community

- Elected to Senior and Junior Honor Societies, high school

- Won varsity tennis letter, 2 years; basketball letter, 2 years

WORK EXPERIENCE

- **Cabaret Director,** University of Alabama, Huntsville
  September, 1990, to February, 1992

  Scheduled bands, comedians, and other talent acts for university performances. Negotiated contracts, prices, arrangements; handled details for university; supervised productions; hosted artists and performers. Attended regional and national Student Activities conventions.

- **Self-employed Leather-crafter**, 1985 through 1992

  Filled custom orders for leather goods (wholesale and retail). Sold several large orders to local specialty shops.

- **Bartender,** T.G.I. Friday's, Huntsville, Alabama, 1991-1993

  Earned college tuition and expense money with part-time work; later promoted to full-time status.

One-page combination resume highlights what was done rather than where he worked. Emphasizes accomplishments over job titles and dates of employment. Approach works to his benefit because it allows him to present strengths.

Stephen H. Zigman • 1458 Rockford Avenue South • Springfield, Maine 11342
(207) 555-7845 • Alternative phone: (207) 555-9613 for messages

Job Objective: Manufacturer's Representative for Audio-Stereo Products

Uses summary to present overview of abilities. Can be quite effective.

Summary:
Set all-new store sales records at Springfield's leading audio equipment retailer for 1990-1994. Sold $1,000,000+ in audio lines. Promoted to manager in June, 1994.

Accomplishments:

Use of "bullets" can call attention to items in a list.

- Won Fisher regional sales award, 1992, for being top salesperson in state

- Awarded trip to Chicago for Customer Electronics Show, June, 1992, by JBL for excellence in speaker sales in 1991

- Developed sales lead and follow-up system used by store for improving sales; store sales increased 44% over prior year

- Graduated with honors from marketing program, Ogunquit Community College, 1989

- Soldier of the Month, Fort Sumter, May, 1986

- Active church member, usher, on committees for several church-related groups

- Was Big Brother to young man for three years, 1991-1993, for Big Brothers of America

- Member, Toastmasters Clubs of America, local chapter; winner of several local awards for public speaking

Employment History:

Short descriptions of work history details give employers helpful information. Use this unless there are job gaps or other problems.

February, 1990, to Present:
Audio Perfection, 2000 Main Street, Springfield, Maine

June, 1987, to February, 1990:
Zigman Contractors, 3652 Third Street, Springfield, Maine (father's company: worked as laborer, helper, carpenter)

June, 1984, to June, 1987:
U.S. Army, radio communications specialist

Education:

Education section on bottom because of significant work experience.

- Ogunquit Community College, 1987-1989
  Graduated with Associate Degree in Business Administration

- Springfield High School
  Graduated in upper 1/3 of class, June, 1984

David W. Browne

1546 Lindwall Terrace
Northbrook, Illinois 60062
(312) 555-6144 (home)
(312) 555-0004 (office)

BACKGROUND SUMMARY

Fifteen years of management-level experience in materials planning, manufacturing, warehousing, distribution, traffic, and facilities planning

EMPLOYMENT HISTORY

1977
to
Present

Worldwide Healthcare Products
Schaumburg, Illinois

1988 to Present   Operations Manager

- Created, developed, and installed new conveyor system. Resulted in savings of $75,000 per year.

- Planned and implemented office and warehouse layouts for both expanding and new facilities.
- Prepared budget of $1.6 million for 30 corporate pharmacy branches in U.S. Control all capital spending for same 30 locations.

- Developed computer program to monitor costs at all locations for 30,000+ orders monthly.

1985 to 1988   Planning Manager

- Designed and opened new Home Patient Distribution Centers. Chose inventory, trained all personnel. All projects completed on time and within budgets.

- Developed, wrote, and published turnkey Startup Manual for opening all new branches.

1982 to 1985   Patient Service Operations Manager

- Opened and managed company's first Home Care facility. Supervised 12 employees.

- Recommended and installed new inventory system to process 50% order-volume increase with no increase in number of employees.

- Designed and opened company's next three Home Care facilities. Wrote and published first Policy and Procedures Manual.

EMPLOYMENT HISTORY (continued)

<u>1977 to 1982</u>	**Training Manager; Int'l. Distribution Manager; On-Site Plant Production Analyst; Inventory Analyst**
1976 to 1977	**Franklin Home Systems** Muncie, Indiana
	Material Control Foreman

EDUCATION AND TRAINING

- Bachelor of Science degree in Business Administration, Ball State University, Muncie, Indiana, June, 1972

- Certificates: "Quality Control & Zero Defects" Crosby Quality College

  "Problem Solving" Kepner-Tregoe Management Institute

PERSONAL INFORMATION

Some say these Personal Information "extras" are unnecessary. The family and church entries imply stability, however, and may have been important in his successful job hunt.

- Married, 2 children; excellent health; willing to travel

- Hobbies: running, all sports, home repair projects

- Elected to Church Council, 800-member congregation

- Member, Council of Logistics Management; Member, Warehouse Education and Research Council

REFERENCES

- Personal and business references are available and will be furnished on request.

Virginia Haskell Gordon
4467A 19th Avenue South
Des Moines, Iowa 50301
(219) 555-6639 (home)
(219) 555-4868 (leave message)

Job Objective: Legal Assistant

EDUCATION

Des Moines Community College, Des Moines, Iowa
Diploma in Paralegal Studies
Graduated with honors in June, 1994

Storm Lake High School, Storm Lake, Iowa
Graduated May, 1972
B+ average; ranked in upper 20% of class

EXPERIENCE

March, 1991
to
August, 1994

Blue Line Temporary Services
Des Moines, Iowa

Temporary-help assignments included:

Legal Secretary:
Worked in eleven law offices, ranging in size from 1 to 47 attorneys. Performed all office duties: type 75 wpm, shorthand, operate legal software and word processing equipment, answer phone, act as receptionist. Familiar with briefs, legal terminology, court documents, correspondent firms, transcripts, etc.

Radio Traffic Clerk
Scheduled commercial radio spots for air time. Took instruction from advertising agencies and program director. Acted as liaison with on-air personalities.

Secretary to Sales Manager
Took minutes and notes at all sales meetings. Typed all correspondence, including confidential business material. Acted as hostess and conducted office tours for visiting executives and clients.

WORK EXPERIENCE (continued)

Large unemployment gap not explained. Most employers will assume time off for raising a family.

June, 1972
to
October, 1987

Meils Ford-Lincoln-Mercury
Storm Lake, Iowa

Secretary-Receptionist/Office Manager
Performed all secretarial and office duties for small-town auto dealership. Typed letters, completed weekly and monthly reports. Answered phones. Handled some sales inquiries. Worked with accountant to complete all financial statements and reports. Did billing and bookkeeping.

PERSONAL INFORMATION

Entries show productivity during time not employed in wage-paying job.

- Married, 3 grown children

- Elected vice-president, Paralegal Club (college); arranged for speakers; planned Chicago trip

- Active in church and school activities; past president, Wilson School PTA

- Enjoy skiing, flower arranging, reading, current events discussion groups

- Volunteer, Breadbasket Food Pantry for homeless

Amanda Perez
N43 W2716 Highway G
Curran, Illinois 60542
(813) 555-3242 (residence)
(813) 555-3555 (answering service)

Job Objective: Sales Representative for
Pharmaceutical Manufacturer/Distributor

WORK EXPERIENCE

<u>MARKETING</u>

- Managed $350,000 marketing campaign for church fund drive. Achieved 12% increase in gifts/pledges.

- Organized volunteer sales force; used demographic data to assign sales team.

- Wrote series of sales letters. Conducted planning meetings, set target dates, delegated follow-up responsibilities. Assisted in training teams on scripts, presentations, "asking for the order."

- Organized new volunteer program for community hospital: gift shop, front desk, readers, sitters, etc. Recruited and maintained initial volunteer corps at 32 people; added 30 people in next twelve months.

EMPLOYMENT HISTORY

- 1979-Present: Registered Nurse, Cole County Hospital Cardiac Care and Intensive Care Units.

- 1975-1979: Medical Assistant, Stephen Brey, M.D. Assisted with routine medical tasks supervised by registered nurse and physician.

EDUCATION

- Bachelor of Science degree in Nursing
  Missouri Western University
  Degree awarded June, 1979; GPA 3.42/4.0

- Medical Assistant Certificate
  Cole County Community College
  Graduated May, 1976; GPA 3.75/4.0

  George Carson High School, diploma, 1974
  Fortuna, Missouri

PERSONAL INFORMATION

- Drive own car; willing to travel overnight; excellent health

- Received $500 annual scholarship from Women's League for five years ($2,500 total) for post-high-school education

JENNIFER LYNN OLSON
4842 Lombard Court
Chicago, Illinois 60608
(312) 555-6864

Job Objective: Beautician/Cosmetologist

EDUCATION

International Beauty Academy
406 North Wabash Avenue
Chicago, Illinois 60606
Graduated from 1-year course in June, 1994

Wilbur Wright College, Chicago
Completed one-year of liberal arts studies

Carl Schurz High School, Chicago
Graduated in June, 1992; "B" grade average

WORK EXPERIENCE

- <u>Completed six-week internship in cosmetology</u> at North-Clark Beauty Studios, Chicago, Illinois. Received all "excellent" ratings and evaluations from beauticians and supervisors. Spring, 1994.

- <u>Supermarket Checker at Smartway Food Market,</u> 3650 North Clark Street, Chicago. Earned funds for all tuition and expenses for college and beauty school plus money for rent, clothes, personal items. Received commendations from Store Manager for good performance and for receiving customer compliments. September, 1991 to Present.

- <u>Babysitter for neighborhood families.</u> Supervised and cared for children 2-8 years old. Also did some house cleaning duties for these families as needed.

COMMUNITY AND SCHOOL ACTIVITIES

- Member, Northside Swing Choir, all three years. Sang in all concerts; participated in choir trips.

- Member, Future Business Leaders of America.

- Lab Assistant, Typing Class.

- Participated in intramural sports.

- Elected secretary, church youth group, senior year. Active member of group throughout high school.

REFERENCES

- References and recommendations are available and will be forwarded on request.

Kevin Wong
4350 Highland Avenue
Tucson, Arizona 85772
(602) 555-7876
(602) 555-2232 (message service)

Job Objective: Electronics Technician

EDUCATION

Arizona Electronics & Technical Institute
Phoenix, Arizona
Associate Degree in Electronics Technology
Grade point average: 3.56 on 4.0 scale
Graduated June, 1995; courses included:

- Digital Electronics
- Microprocessors
- Circuit Design
- Hands-on Repair

- AF & RF Analog Electronics
- Fabrication
- Design Applications
- Communications

Tucson North High School
Honors Grades in Math, Science, and Drawing
Received diploma in May, 1993

WORK EXPERIENCE

- Unified Telephone Company
  Tucson, Arizona

  Responsible for troubleshooting and repairing various types of telephones, including cordless, dial, Touch-Tone, and full-feature desk phones.

  Worked from September, 1993, to Present.

- Bob's Big Boy Restaurant
  Tucson, Arizona

  Busboy, Waiter. Commended as "one of my best workers" by restaurant manager.

  Worked two years, part-time after school.

SCHOOL AND COMMUNITY ACTIVITIES

- Member, Math Club, Kit Car Club, Letterman's Club

- Assistant coach for Cub Scout Baseball Team

Ronald P. Andrews
1437 Richer Avenue
East Town, Maryland 21602
(805) 555-8943
Leave message: 555-6562

Job Objective: Computer Repair Technician

EDUCATION

International Computer Institute
Washington, D.C.
Diploma in Computer Repair, June, 1994
Completed 18-month training program; "B" average

Walter Raleigh High School
East Town, Maryland
Graduated in June, 1991

WORK HISTORY

September, 1992
to
Present

Ardata Computer Systems: "The Computer Store"
Washington, D.C.

Troubleshoot and repair IBM-compatible MS-DOS computer systems, including hard disk drives; dot-matrix, inkjet, and laser printers; laptop portables and desktop models.

Familiar with various brands of equipment; able to diagnose simple or complex malfunctions. Read schematic diagrams. Enjoy mechanical as well as electronic work. Worked part-time to earn tuition and expense money for computer school.

June, 1990
to
September, 1992

CopyQuick Instant Printers
East Town, Maryland

Computer clerk and printer at instant print shop. Waited on customers. Advised on paper, ink, quantities, paper selection, binding. Ran printing equipment for hundreds of different types of print jobs, including multi-color work. Worked after school and weekends as needed.

MEMBERSHIPS, CLUBS, AND ACTIVITIES

- Varsity baseball team, Letterman's Club officer

- Member, Electronics Club, Ham Radio Club

- Volunteer Camp Counselor, summer church camp.

Jerry P. Longarrow
2961 Passmore Circle
Tulsa, Oklahoma 74196.
(303) 555-2349

Job Objective: Retail Men's Clothing Salesperson

EDUCATION

Maxwell High School
Maxwell, Kansas
"B" Average; upper 40% of class
Graduated, June, 1995

- Received A's and B's in Marketing Education Classes

- Took college preparatory subjects: algebra, English, sociology, and psychology, plus business subjects: accounting, economics, business law, marketing, and salesmanship.

- Won regional and state prizes in marketing competitions, 1995

WORK EXPERIENCE

- September, 1993, to Present

  Edgar's Men's Wear
  Maxwell, Kansas

  Salesman for Men's Wear Store

  Worked after school and weekends in full-line men's wear retail store in city of 35,000. Sold suits, sport coats, shirts, ties, and all related types of clothing and accessories. Average sales of $1,000 per 40-hour week. Developed own customers. Eligible for rehire.

  After first year, Mr. William Edgar also asked me to work full-time in summer. "You've done excellent work, Jerry, and we want you with us full-time."

PERSONAL INFORMATION

- Currently attending Tulsa Junior College studying marketing and business

- Excellent health; active in sports and fitness

- Member, Maxwell Drum & Bugle Band (trumpet)

- Business and personal references are available and will be furnished on request

DOUGLAS J. ST. JOHN
4452 Dayton Drive
College Park, Illinois 60011
(609) 555-9821

JOB OBJECTIVE: Sales Representative for food or toiletry products
to retail grocery and drug outlets

EDUCATION

Bachelor of Arts degree in English
Graduated, June, 1994
Salisbury State University
Steakville, Iowa

Diploma in College Preparatory Studies, 1990
Leonard Birdwhistle High School
Duluth, Minnesota

> One-page resume for recent graduate. It highlights his activities on campus—his best selling point. He could have instead started with a "WORK EXPERIENCE" section and told more about his Super-Valu Market summer job. But his leadership items are stronger, and he properly leads off with them.
>
> His work is slightly related to his chosen job objective; that should help!

HONORS, AWARDS, AND ACHIEVEMENTS

- Elected President, Associated Student Board of Governors, Salisbury State University, 1992-93

- Selected for Dean's List, all semesters; 3.8 grade average required

- Homecoming Court, Junior Year

- Selected for "Lyre's Club," Senior Honorary for Marching Band

- Vice-President, Pi Kappa Alpha social fraternity, 1992-93

- Vice-President, "Student Advertising and Sales Management Club"

PERSONAL INFORMATION

- Worked three summers for Super-Valu Market, Duluth, Minnesota; promoted to supervisor of all stockers for final summer of employment

- Earned funds for college expenses, working as audiovisual technician for various events on campus; paid 85% of all college costs

- Enjoy all sports, intramural athletics, physical fitness

- Have traveled throughout United States with parents and family

- Member, church youth group in high school and college

REFERENCES

- School, business, and personal references are available and will be furnished on request

DOUGLAS J. ST. JOHN
4452 Dayton Drive
College Park, Illinois 60011
(609) 555-9821

JOB OBJECTIVE: Sales Representative for food or toiletry products to retail grocery and drug outlets

EDUCATION

Bachelor of Arts degree in English
Graduated, June, 1994
Salisbury State University
Steakville, Iowa

This version of Doug's resume is exactly the same as the first except that the headings are slightly larger. Which version do you like better? Does the change in heading size make any difference? Experiment with several sizes to see which size looks best for your resume!

Diploma in College Preparatory Studies, 1990
Leonard Birdwhistle High School
Duluth, Minnesota

HONORS, AWARDS, AND ACHIEVEMENTS

- Elected President, Associated Student Board of Governors, Salisbury State University, 1992-93

- Selected for Dean's List, all semesters; 3.8 grade average required

- Homecoming Court, Junior Year

- Selected for "Lyre's Club," Senior Honorary for Marching Band

- Vice-President, Pi Kappa Alpha social fraternity, 1992-93

- Vice-President, "Student Advertising and Sales Management Club"

PERSONAL INFORMATION

- Worked three summers for Super-Valu Market, Duluth, Minnesota; promoted to supervisor of all stockers for final summer of employment

- Earned funds for college expenses, working as audiovisual technician for various events on campus; paid 85% of all college costs

- Enjoy all sports, intramural athletics, physical fitness

- Have traveled throughout United States with parents and family

- Member, church youth group in high school and college

REFERENCES

- School, business, and personal references are available and will be furnished on request

Brett Alan Christopher

785 Minnetonka Court
Edina, Minnesota
(612) 555-2096

Job Objective: A Marketing Opportunity

encompassing some research and analysis, extensive customer contact,
and in-person personal sales of travel-related consumer products or services

Education

Normandale Community College
Associate of Arts degree, May, 1992
Majoring in Pre-Law and Business Administration
3.25/4.0 GPA

Edina High School
Graduated in Upper 10% of class
Honor Student, 3.5/4.0 GPA
Diploma received June, 1989

Activities, Awards, and Honors

- Captain, Normandale Community College Varsity Soccer Team

- Elected Most Valuable Player, Varsity Soccer Team, 1990

- Member, Student Governing Board, Normandale Community College

- Member, Activities & Events Selection Committee, NCC

- Selected to represent college at Midwest Region convention for National Association for Campus Activities (NACA)

- Coaching Assistant, Varsity Soccer team, 1991

- Won Varsity Letter in Fencing, Edina High School

- Member, Cross-Country Skiing Racing Team; top skier, finished 1st and 2nd; fastest in school of 2,500

- Member, Varsity Track team, 2 years (pole vault)

- Member, Varsity Swimming Team

- Official School Photographer, newspaper and yearbook

Community Activities

- Selected as Tutor/Peer Counselor for YMCA, 1987-1989

- Chosen to compete in National Graphic Arts Competition for two consecutive years

It's not cool these days to indicate height, weight, birth date, etc., but if you think they help your case, I think there's nothing wrong with them. They may, in certain circumstances, be politically incorrect, so judge wisely in adding or omitting these.

PERSONAL INFORMATION

- Born March 9, 1971; 6 feet tall, 155 pounds; excellent health and physical condition

- Selected as "Man of the Year" model/athlete to represent Minnesota in national Atlantic City male-model competition

- Have traveled widely throughout United States, Caribbean area, Mexico, England, Germany, Switzerland, Austria

- Paid all college tuition and expenses by working part-time since age 16 (waiter, photo proofer, printer, selling men's clothing, etc.)

- Professional model; completed training at John Robert Powers School in May, 1990

EMPLOYMENT HISTORY

"Student jobs" and other part-time jobs don't deserve much detail unless they entail some trust and responsibility and are directly related to the field you want to enter after graduation. For example, working in a hospital or pharmacy could give you an edge for a pharmaceutical sales job.

- 1991-Present

  Charlie's Restaurant
  Bloomington, Minnesota
  Waiter

- 1989-1991

  Print-Graphics, Inc.
  Minneapolis, Minnesota
  Color Proofer; Printing Coordinator

- 1988-1989

  Bowman's (men's clothing store)
  Minneapolis, Minnesota
  Retail sales of men's accessories

- 1987-1989

  YMCA
  Edina, Minnesota
  Speaker; selected as "Teen Peer Educator"
  (Tutor for other high school students);
  taught various subjects as needed

REFERENCES

- Business, personal, and educational references are available and will be furnished on request.

Is this necessary? Some resume books are now saying to leave it out. It's still a part of most resumes because it implies that you're not afraid to have some checking done on yourself and that people are willing to say nice things about you.

CRAIG R. JENSEN
155 Warrenton Terrace
Omaha, Nebraska 68173
(402) 555-4949

EMPLOYMENT HISTORY

September, 1983
to
July, 1994

Sun Community & Suburban Newspapers
Omaha, Nebraska

1992-1994   **Coordinator, Shows & Exhibits**

- Planned, directed, and coordinated two annual 4-day exhibit-shows: Home Interiors Show; and Lawn, Garden & Landscape Show. Each event budgeted at $100,000 and showed profit of 20 percent.

- Sold concepts and exhibit space to local, regional and national firms. Supervised and managed sales activities of 10 full-time salespeople. Increased shows from one annually to three in 1993.

- Coordinated all advertising and marketing for shows: broadcast, print, and outdoor. Created ideas, wrote scripts, and produced and directed audio and video commercials. Created, wrote, and produced print advertisements and promotional literature.

- Developed show design-concepts, themes, layouts, displays, and exhibits. Worked with designers and professional exhibit firms.

- Interviewed and selected qualified professionals for show seminars and lectures.

- Acted as Master of Ceremonies for all shows; audiences exceeded 500 people per seminar.

1988-1992   **Senior Advertising Sales Executive**

- Created, designed, and wrote copy for advertisements in 15 weekly papers serving suburbs of Omaha.

- Sold new advertising and marketing programs and special sections. Developed concepts for 35 sections/supplements annually.

- Increased lowest-production sales territory to second place among all regions; increased actual territorial sales volume by 300 percent over quota.

> Craig has worked for one employer for most of his lifetime employment. This method of dates-for-each-job is a good way to handle this situation.
>
> Notice how the numbers pop out of Craig's "Results and Accomplishments" section. You should make a special effort to **quantify whatever you can!**

• Set all-time sales record for company in newly split sales region. Sold $500,000+ in print ads.

WORK EXPERIENCE (continued)

1983-1988   **Graphic Production Assistant**

Craig was born in 1967, so his high school record gets very little space, even though it is impressive.

When you're nearing, or over, age 30, employers are more interested in your recent results-and-accomplishments and not as much in what you did at age 16-17. But even there, the numbers are impressive and help his case. (He's now selling computer software to doctors' offices and doing very well.)

• Hired as mail room worker, then promoted into various positions of increasing responsibility for this 35-year-old, 200-employee corporation (division of World Media, Seattle, Washington).

• Laid out advertisements for all papers; operated production cameras and web presses. Selected for apprenticeship program in graphic arts.

• Redesigned, supervised, and redecorated offices at corporate headquarters; increased workflow productivity and efficiency.

ACHIEVEMENTS AND HONORS

• President of Student Council and Junior Class in suburban high school of 1,700 students; Captain, Varsity Swimming Team; letterman, three years; raised $2,000 for class fund; Honor Roll.

• Selected for two-week missionary project in West Indies, 1984

EDUCATION

• University of Nebraska, Class of 1988
  Major: Marketing and Business Administration
  Senior Standing; GPA 3.0/4.0

PERSONAL INFORMATION

• Born 1967; 5 feet, 10 inches tall; 165 pounds

• Enjoy running, sports, aerobic exercise, music, theatre, reading

• Have traveled widely throughout United States, Europe, Canada, Bahamas, West Indies

REFERENCES

• Business and personal references are available and will gladly be furnished on request.

SCOTT W. KIERNAN

2100 Hollyhock Lane
Oak Forest, Illinois 60452
(708) 555-0522 home; (312) 555-4461 office

PROFESSIONAL EXPERIENCE

1991 to Present	**ILLINOIS BANK CORPORATION** Chicago, Illinois

Vice President, Financial Services Group

- Promoted to VP while $40-billion bank system was downsizing and restructuring. Personally responsible for $2.2 million in annual profits.

- Managed all marketing and sales programs for $70 million (average) student loan portfolio. Responsible for profit and loss. Sell $50-$60 million in educational student loans annually.

- Purchase and sell loans. Negotiate all service/sale contracts. Supervise 14 people: coordinators, assistant, loan servicers. Plan, control, and authorize disbursements: $3-million annual budget.

1988 to 1991	**Assistant Vice President/Manager** **Financial Services Group**

- Manage marketing and sales programs for student loans. Sold all retail products and services, including home equity lines of credit. Supervised 13 persons.

1986 to 1988	**Officer, Financial Services Group**

- Sold all retail investment products and services; emphasis on insurance, annuities, and Qualified Retirement Sales.

1964 to 1986	**Marketing Representative**

- Planned and executed all marketing strategies for out-of-state solicitations in student lending.

- Made in-person sales calls to universities in seven states; conducted telemarketing research and sales training programs; purchased loans from financial institutions; developed projections on profitability of loan portfolios.

1982 to 1984	**Commercial Service Representative** (Illinois Bank Corporation)

Scott Kiernan   Page 2

PROFESSIONAL EXPERIENCE (continued)

KEY ACCOMPLISHMENTS

- Achieved more than 1.50 percent return on assets and 30 percent return on equity through stringent and prudent portfolio management

- Planned and helped organize "Legislative Symposium of the Higher Education Act" with Senators and Congressmen on program

- Awarded "Certified Financial Planner" (CFP) designation in 1993

- Negotiated/closed $245-million contract with Student Loan Marketing Association

- #1 lender of student loans in Illinois; portfolio grew from $200,000 to $90-million

- Sold $5 million+ of insurance products and annuities in 30 months

- Won two national sales contests; placed in "Top Three" in third contest, all since 1993 (conducted by Illinois Bank Insurance Co.)

- Successfully completed "Commercial Lending School," 1990, and "Professional Selling Skills," 1989

- Won "Marketing Achievement Award" for account reps, 1986

EDUCATION

If someone were hiring only MBA's, we might move this Education section to the beginning of the resume so that the reader would be sure to see the section right away.

- Master of Business Administration
  University of Chicago, Chicago, Illinois
  Awarded May, 1991; GPA: 3.6/4.0

- Bachelor of Science in Business Administration—Finance
  University of Illinois—Champaign
  Awarded May, 1987; GPA: 3.2/4.0

PROFESSIONAL AND CIVIC ORGANIZATIONS

- Member, Sales and Marketing Executives of Metropolitan Chicago

- Member, numerous regional, state, and national financial aid organizations

- Member, high school "Partners for Progress" Program; mentor for St. George High School students, Chicago

INTERESTS

- Enjoy all sports, hunting, fishing, photography, travel, and reading business publications

Scott W. Kiernan

The list of references is an
addendum. He can include it
or omit it when he sends or
brings the resume. Note that
the reference information is
complete (addresses, phone
numbers, etc.), making it very
easy to contact references.

REFERENCES

Mr. Richard Johnston
President
Midwest Guarantor Services, Inc.
850 North Huey Place, Suite 6
Cleveland, Ohio 44109-2172
(210) 555-7661

Mr. Ralph Dousman
Director, Office of Student Financial Services
University of Illinois
432 North Iroquois Street
Champaign, Illinois 61820-1496
(301) 263-3202

Mr. Rolland Houghton
President
Illinois Bank—Kankakee
4200 West White Deer Road
Kankakee, Illinois 60901-4470
(301) 555-3341

Ms. Roberta James
Fortunato Securities Group, Inc.
Executive Vice President and Director of Corporate Finance
110 North LaSalle Street
Chicago, Illinois 60606
(312) 555-3400

Mr. Terrence Tagliaferro
President
Illinois Financial Guarantee, Inc.
6 West Dearborn Street, Suite 1910
Schlepman Tower
Chicago, Illinois 60606
(312) 555-3786

BLAKE ALAN POTTER
716 North Louis Avenue
Hood River, Oregon 97744
(503) 555-0530

Job Objective: Banquet Manager

PROFESSIONAL PROFILE

We could have called this profile—at the beginning—a "Summary" instead. It points out his job objective nicely, along with his current job information and experience.

- Experienced in all phases of hotel/resort banquet management
- Highly organized and dedicated with cheerful, positive attitude
- Effective problem-solver; attentive to detail

WORK EXPERIENCE

1980 to Present

Mountaintop Resort
Hood River, Oregon

Banquet Manager

This wide margin isn't "wasted space." It aids readability greatly.

- Manage, supervise, and train 20-60 employees of 320-room resort and convention facility.

- Set up rooms and serviced guests for conventions, weddings, theme parties, special events, banquets, off-premise catering, and seminars for groups of 12 to 2,000 people.

- Established improved policies and procedures resulting in increased efficiency and productivity in dealing with employees and customers.

- Prepare weekly forecasts, yearly budgets, profit projections, and all financial data for banquet department.

- Developed and implemented new banquet and bar training manuals.

- Established new and highly successful custom themes for parties and conventions, all easily set up and implemented by banquet staff

- Developed creative new banquet menus and wine lists; work with local vendors and suppliers to develop exclusive products.

- Increased banquet sales from $190,000 in 1983 to $900,000 in 1990.

SEMINARS

- "Banquet Management," National Restaurant Association

- "Interpersonal Skills," Northwest Community College

- "Hospitality/Impression Creating Seminar" by James Garfield

- "Bar and Beverage Management," National Restaurant Association

- "Increasing Profits in Food & Beverage Operations," National Restaurant Association

EDUCATION

- Lane Community College, Eugene, Oregon, 1980

- South Portland High School, Portland, Oregon, 1979

REFERENCES

- Business and personal references and letters of recommendation are available and will be furnished on request.

ZACK R. NALLMAN
4478 NW Taylor Street
Jacksonville, Florida 32230
(904) 555-7877

This resume could easily have been put on one page but would have lost readability. Don't fall victim to the "it shouldn't be longer than one page" myth. Most important (I know you're tired of hearing this now), make it readable!

HOTEL MANAGEMENT ASSISTANT OR TRAINEE

WORK EXPERIENCE

Summer, 1994

Inn of the Plantation
Jacksonville, Florida

Front Desk Manager Trainee

The bullet that precedes each item points the eye and says, "Start reading here." Bullets help the reader scan through your resume easily.

- Answered phones, solved guest problems and conflicts, checked in guests at four-star premier resort hotel (540 rooms). Condominium-and-hotel property. Took reservations. Worked in all front office areas. Used computer system for entire property operations. Assisted guests in planning activities. Sold trip packages, sports programs, horseback riding, other resort events.

Summer, 1993

Las Vegas Athletic Club
Las Vegas, Nevada

Front Desk Attendant

- Worked at front desk of largest private club in Las Vegas, including hotel and athletic facilities. Checked in guests, allocated rooms. Used desktop computer system for reservations, operations, etc.

Summer, 1992

Inn of the Plantation
Jacksonville, Florida

Caterer/Banquet Waiter

- Served and worked with traditional resort clientele, including conventions, meetings, banquets, and family/restaurant trade. Worked with Banquet Manager to plan, set up, and take down banquets and special events for parties of 6 to 500.

February, 1992
to
June, 1992

Nimitz Memorial Hospital
Jacksonville, Florida

Dietary Aide

- Served patients and prepared meals, including special dietary meals (Kosher, vegetarian, low sodium, etc.)

EDUCATION

- Bachelor of Science degree in Hotel Management
  University of Florida, Gainesville
  Date of graduation: June, 1995; honor student
  Attended and graduated on academic scholarship

LEADERSHIP ACTIVITIES, HONORS, AND AWARDS

- President, Eta Sigma Delta (Hotel Honorary), 1994-95
  Vice-President, 1993-94

- Chairman, University of Florida 1994 Hospitality Auction

- Elected officer, Sigma Chi fraternity, 1993-94

- Awarded "William Johnson Scholarship," 1993

- Awarded "Schielein Scholarship" for Hotel Management Excellence, 1994

- Member, Lacrosse Team, 1992, 1993, 1994

- Member, Hotel Restaurant Tourism Society, 1992, 1993, 1994

- Worked on successful Sales Blitz for Ritz-Carlton Hotels, spring, 1994; called 100+ prospective clients and meeting planners; worked with Ritz-Carlton Hotel sales managers

- President, Student Body, Sunriver High School

- Captain, Varsity Football Team, Sunriver High School; selected for all-conference team, 1990

- Captain, Varsity Basketball Team, Sunriver High School; honorable mention for all-conference

- Letterman, Varsity Football, Basketball, and Track teams

- Elected Senator, Florida Boys State, 1990; ran mock government, including legislature, with/for selected Florida high school students

> What if you don't have all these great activities and offices?
>
> Make the most of what you do have. First, write down on your rough draft everything you've done or been in. Then eliminate the least-impressive items. You'll be left with the best ones. You should arrange those in the order of their importance from most important to least important. (If you have to eliminate some of these because you're out of space, you can knock out the ones at the bottom.)

HOME ADDRESS

- P.O. Box 35
  Sunriver, Florida 32211
  (904) 555-2362

> If you're living away at school, you should have your permanent (home) address and phone number somewhere on your resume. You want readers to be able to contact you, so you should do what's necessary (have an answering machine; coach your roommates to answer properly; tell your wife, kids, and parents about your resume; etc.). You'd be surprised at how many people miss the chance for an interview because they weren't home when we called or were otherwise unable to be contacted. If we try three times without success, we do what you probably would do: give up.

REFERENCES

- Business and personal references are available and will be furnished on request.

JARED G. WILLIAMS

9875 North Port Sound Road
Falmouth, Massachusetts 02540
(617) 555-2426

Here's a trade school diesel graduate who looks great on paper and should get interviews with this resume. In trade or vocational or career schools, a course listing up front like this (directly-related to his career field) is more important than for a graduate of a liberal-arts college.

Your interest in sports, fishing, hunting, etc., might give the employer something in common to talk about during the interview. It's not job-related, but if you think it may add some flavoring to your resume, go ahead and put it in.

EDUCATION

Global Diesel Training School
Boston, Massachusetts
Graduated June, 1994; 3.2/4.0 grade average

1-year program in Diesel Mechanics; curriculum included these courses:

- Industrial Math I
- Basic Mechanics
- Related Welding I
- Diesel Mechanics
- Applied Psychology

- Algebra
- Hydraulics
- Diesel Principles
- Advanced Diesel Mechanics
- Communication Skills I

Falmouth High School
Falmouth, Massachusetts
Graduated May, 1991
Ranked in upper 1/2 of class

WORK EXPERIENCE

June, 1993
to May, 1994

Global Diesel Training School
Boston, Massachusetts

Shop Assistant

Assist instructors to maintain shop in prime condition for training. Keep log of tools used by students in shop and class. Work part-time 15 hours per week while attending school to help with expenses.

Summers, 1990,
1991, 1992

Peterbilt Trucks of Falmouth
Falmouth, Massachusetts

Shop Assistant

Assisted mechanics on various jobs and tasks. Learned complete methods of mainte-nance and repair from certified mechanics with extensive training from Peterbilt, Kenworth, and other truck manufacturers.

INTERESTS AND ACTIVITIES

- Earned Honor Roll grades at Global Diesel; elected to Student Council

- Enjoy sports, hunting, fishing, swimming

- Member, Auto Mechanics Club in high school

- Participated in regional competitions for Vocational Industrial Clubs of America; won 1st place senior year, 2nd place junior year

- Played all intramural sports in high school

REFERENCES

- Business, school, and personal references are available and will be furnished on request.

JARED G. WILLIAMS
9875 North Port Sound Road
Falmouth, Massachusetts 02540
(617) 555-2426

EDUCATION

Global Diesel Training School
Boston, Massachusetts
Graduated June, 1994; 3.2/4.0 grade average

1-year program in Diesel Mechanics; curriculum included these courses:

- Industrial Math I
- Basic Mechanics
- Related Welding I
- Diesel Mechanics
- Applied Psychology

- Algebra
- Hydraulics
- Diesel Principles
- Advanced Diesel Mechanics
- Communication Skills I

Falmouth High School
Falmouth, Massachusetts
Graduated May, 1991
Ranked in upper 1/2 of class

WORK EXPERIENCE

June, 1993
to May, 1994

Global Diesel Training School
Boston, Massachusetts

Shop Assistant

Assist instructors to maintain shop in prime condition for training. Keep log of tools used by students in shop and class. Work part-time 15 hours per week while attending school to help with expenses.

Summers, 1990,
1991, 1992

Peterbilt Trucks of Falmouth
Falmouth, Massachusetts

Shop Assistant

Assisted mechanics on various jobs and tasks. Learned complete methods of maintenance and repair from certified mechanics with extensive training from Peterbilt, Kenworth, and other truck manufacturers.

INTERESTS AND ACTIVITIES

- Earned Honor Roll grades at Global Diesel; elected to Student Council

- Enjoy sports, hunting, fishing, swimming

- Member, Auto Mechanics Club in high school

- Participated in regional competitions for Vocational Industrial Clubs of America; won 1st place senior year, 2nd place junior year

- Played all intramural sports in high school

REFERENCES

- Business, school, and personal references are available and will be furnished on request.

Grant A. Gallant

1500 Stanton Terrace
Manchester, New Hampshire
(603) 555-9147

Grant has "a whole lot of stuff" in this resume. We recommended that he eliminate some of his material, but he felt that "all of it is important." The resume still works for him because it has narrow columns and bullets (I like this) in front of each item, and because he's been cleverly stingy with his words: each item is s-h-o-r-t !

Background Summary

Executive-level experience in corporate financial planning and analysis, accounting, facilities management, purchasing, mail-center operations, sales promotions, and self-development.

Employment History

1978 to Present

Superior Insurance Company
Manchester, New Hampshire

May, 1989
to Present

Planning and Control Manager
Regional Operations Center, Manchester, New Hampshire
- Responsible for all financial planning and analysis
- Expanded expense accountability by more than 10% (expense budget is $28 million)
- Developed financial models to determine desired staffing reductions
- Established Administrative Division: accounting, data processing, purchasing, quality assurance
- Manage office (160,000 sq. ft.); coordinated $2-million remodeling project
- Directly responsible for staff of 100 employees: 20 salaried and 80 hourly associates

April, 1987
to May, 1989

Administrative Financial Manager
Home Office, Manchester, New Hampshire
- Managed both Premium and Expense Units
- Analyzed results of 28 regional offices
- Provided all financial reports for CEO, COO, etc.
- Provided technical support to field offices; published bulletins
- Completed 60-page "Home Office Expense Plan"
- Developed and made formal presentations to all senior operating officers

May, 1985
to April, 1987

Financial Division Manager
Syracuse Regional Office
- Responsible for all financial planning, operational analysis and budgeting; revenues exceeded $300 million
- Implemented program to generate premiums valued at $5 million
- Developed new "Sales Management Performance Bonus Plan"

May, 1984
to May, 1985

Administrative Division Manager
Syracuse Regional Office
- Established Division following consolidation of Operation Center
- Responsible for sales support, mail and supplies, lease management, purchasing, accounts payable
- Relocated Regional Office and Claims Office from company-owned building to leased location

Employment History (continued)

September, 1982
to May, 1984

Accounting Division Manager
Syracuse Regional Operations Center
- Accountable for monthly and year-end financial reports
- Insured accurate postings to all ledgers
- Processed posting of all payments and funds
- Reconciled all bank accounts
- Successfully passed all audits without errors

July, 1978
to September, 1982

Accounting Supervisor/Unit Manager
[and Management Development Rotation Program (7 mos.)]

Education

- Bachelor of Science degree in Accounting
  University of New Hampshire
  Degree granted: May, 1978

Military

- Major, United States Army Reserve
- Currently assigned as Brigade Logistics Officer
- Prior key assignments as Military Instructor and Company Commander

Personal Information

- Married, 3 children
- Excellent health
- Willing to travel and relocate
- Hobbies: running, racquetball, golf

References

- Personal and Business References are available and will be furnished on request.

Grant A. Gallant
1500 Stanton Terrace
Manchester, New Hampshire
(603) 555-9147

Background Summary

Executive-level experience in corporate financial planning and analysis, accounting, facilities management, purchasing, mail-center operations, sales promotions, and self-development.

Employment History

1978 to Present	**Superior Insurance Company** Manchester, New Hampshire

May, 1989 to Present

Planning and Control Manager
Regional Operations Center, Manchester, New Hampshire
- Responsible for all financial planning and analysis
- Expanded expense accountability by more than 10% (expense budget is $28 million)
- Developed financial models to determine desired staffing reductions
- Established Administrative Division: accounting, data processing, purchasing, quality assurance
- Manage office (160,000 sq. ft.); coordinated $2-million remodeling project
- Directly responsible for staff of 100 employees: 20 salaried and 80 hourly associates

April, 1987 to May, 1989

Administrative Financial Manager
Home Office, Manchester, New Hampshire
- Managed both Premium and Expense Units
- Analyzed results of 28 regional offices
- Provided all financial reports for CEO, COO, etc.
- Provided technical support to field offices; published bulletins
- Completed 60-page "Home Office Expense Plan"
- Developed and made formal presentations to all senior operating officers

May, 1985 to April, 1987

Financial Division Manager
Syracuse Regional Office
- Responsible for all financial planning, operational analysis and budgeting; revenues exceeded $300 million
- Implemented program to generate premiums valued at $5 million
- Developed new "Sales Management Performance Bonus Plan"

Here's the same resume, but we've "bumped up the type size one notch," from 10 points in the first version to 11 points in the second. You can do this with your own resume, too, if you're creating it on a computer with WYSIWYG (what you see is what you get). Try several sizes and see which size is the most readable and still provides plenty of white space.

Employment History (continued)

May, 1984
to May, 1985

Administrative Division Manager
Syracuse Regional Office
- Established Division following consolidation of Operation Center
- Responsible for sales support, mail and supplies, lease management, purchasing, accounts payable
- Relocated Regional Office and Claims Office from company-owned building to leased location

September, 1982
to May, 1984

Accounting Division Manager
Syracuse Regional Operations Center
- Accountable for monthly and year-end financial reports
- Insured accurate postings to all ledgers
- Processed posting of all payments and funds
- Reconciled all bank accounts
- Successfully passed all audits without errors

July, 1978
to September, 1982

Accounting Supervisor/Unit Manager
[and Management Development Rotation Program (7 mos.)]

Education

- Bachelor of Science degree in Accounting
  University of New Hampshire
  Degree granted: May, 1978

Military

- Major, United States Army Reserve
- Currently assigned as Brigade Logistics Officer
- Prior key assignments as Military Instructor and Company Commander

Personal Information

- Married, 3 children
- Excellent health
- Willing to travel and relocate
- Hobbies: running, racquetball, golf

References

- Personal and Business References are available and will be furnished on request.

ALAN G. WALTERS

6603 W. Lloyd Lane
Palatine, Illinois
(708) 555-4598

QUALIFICATIONS SUMMARY

Sales and Marketing Professional with over 20 years in industrial gases and chemicals, including 14 years in Management: bulk, medical gases, carbon dioxide, and related chemicals.

WORK HISTORY

1990 to Present	**Industrial Gas Co., Inc.**, Schaumburg, Illinois **District Manager**

- Managed 8 salespeople; sales budget $12.5 million for 1994. Directed all sales and marketing of IGC's gases in northern Illinois.

- Exceeded 1993 sales goals by 11% in recession economy.

- Contributed $2.5 million in added annual revenue by expanding largest bulk gas account in entire company.

- Administered largest price increase in history of Midwest Region; resulted in more than $200,000 in added revenue.

1983 to 1990	**National Industrial Gas Corporation**, Arlington Heights, Illinois **Sales Manager, Midwest**

- Achieved or exceeded budget all 9 years; $10 million budget for bulk and specialty gases in 1990.

- Supervised 15 offices within 5-state region.

- Managed and supported distribution and technical service departments; 275 bulk gas customers; annual budget: $2 million.

1976 to 1983	**Chemical & Gas Products, Inc.**, Oak Brook, Illinois **Product Manager, Midwest**

- Managed specialty/medical gas products/carbon dioxide with total budget $9 million. Achieved 117% of sales goals.

- Ranked in top 25% of all region salespeople for all 7 years; promoted to Regional Product Manager in 1981.

1972 to 1976	**Pennsylvania Minerals, Inc.**, Harrisburg, Pennsylvania **Sales Representative, Pennsylvania**

- Managed largest sales territory ($6 million) in region. Developed USX Corporation into $2-million-dollar account.

ALAN G. WALTERS
6603 W. Lloyd Lane
Palatine, Illinois
(708) 555-4598

QUALIFICATIONS SUMMARY

Sales and Marketing Professional with over 20 years in industrial gases and chemicals, including 14 years in Management: bulk, medical gases, carbon dioxide, and related chemicals.

WORK HISTORY

1990 to Present   **Industrial Gas Co., Inc.**, Schaumburg, Illinois
District Manager

- Managed 8 salespeople; sales budget $12.5 million for 1994. Directed all sales and marketing of IGC's gases in northern Illinois.

- Exceeded 1993 sales goals by 11% in recession economy.

- Contributed $2.5 million in added annual revenue by expanding largest bulk gas account in entire company.

- Administered largest price increase in history of Midwest Region; resulted in more than $200,000 in added revenue.

1983 to 1990   **National Industrial Gas Corporation**, Arlington Heights, Illinois
Sales Manager, Midwest

- Achieved or exceeded budget all 9 years; $10 million budget for bulk and specialty gases in 1990.

- Supervised 15 offices within 5-state region.

- Managed and supported distribution and technical service departments; 275 bulk gas customers; annual budget: $2 million.

1976 to 1983   **Chemical & Gas Products, Inc.**, Oak Brook, Illinois
Product Manager, Midwest

- Managed specialty/medical gas products/carbon dioxide with total budget $9 million. Achieved 117% of sales goals.

- Ranked in top 25% of all region salespeople for all 7 years; promoted to Regional Product Manager in 1981.

1972 to 1976   **Pennsylvania Minerals, Inc.**, Harrisburg, Pennsylvania
Sales Representative, Pennsylvania

- Managed largest sales territory ($6 million) in region. Developed USX Corporation into $2-million-dollar account.

ALAN G. WALTERS
6603 W. Lloyd Lane
Palatine, Illinois
(708) 555-4598

QUALIFICATIONS SUMMARY

Sales and Marketing Professional with over 20 years in industrial gases and chemicals, including 14 years in Management: bulk, medical gases, carbon dioxide, and related chemicals.

WORK HISTORY

1990 to Present

Industrial Gas Co., Inc., Schaumburg, Illinois
District Manager

- Managed 8 salespeople; sales budget $12.5 million for 1994. Directed all sales and marketing of IGC's gases in northern Illinois.

- Exceeded 1993 sales goals by 11% in recession economy.

- Contributed $2.5 million in added annual revenue by expanding largest bulk gas account in entire company.

- Administered largest price increase in history of Midwest Region; resulted in more than $200,000 in added revenue.

1983 to 1990

National Industrial Gas Corporation, Arlington Heights, Illinois
Sales Manager, Midwest

- Achieved or exceeded budget all 9 years; $10 million budget for bulk and specialty gases in 1990.

- Supervised 15 offices within 5-state region.

- Managed and supported distribution and technical service departments; 275 bulk gas customers; annual budget: $2 million.

1976 to 1983

Chemical & Gas Products, Inc., Oak Brook, Illinois
Product Manager, Midwest

- Managed specialty/medical gas products/carbon dioxide with total budget $9 million. Achieved 117% of sales goals.

- Ranked in top 25% of all region salespeople for all 7 years; promoted to Regional Product Manager in 1981.

1972 to 1976

Pennsylvania Minerals, Inc., Harrisburg, Pennsylvania
Sales Representative, Pennsylvania

- Managed largest sales territory ($6 million) in region. Developed USX Corporation into $2-million-dollar account.

ALAN G. WALTERS
6603 W. Lloyd Lane
Palatine, Illinois
(708) 555-4598

QUALIFICATIONS SUMMARY

Sales and Marketing Professional with over 20 years in industrial gases and chemicals, including 14 years in Management: bulk, medical gases, carbon dioxide, and related chemicals.

WORK HISTORY

1990 to Present **Industrial Gas Co., Inc.**, Schaumburg, Illinois
District Manager

- Managed 8 salespeople; sales budget $12.5 million for 1994. Directed all sales and marketing of IGC's gases in northern Illinois.

- Exceeded 1993 sales goals by 11% in recession economy.

- Contributed $2.5 million in added annual revenue by expanding largest bulk gas account in entire company.

- Administered largest price increase in history of Midwest Region; resulted in more than $200,000 in added revenue.

1983 to 1990 **National Industrial Gas Corporation**, Arlington Heights, Illinois
Sales Manager, Midwest

- Achieved or exceeded budget all 9 years; $10 million budget for bulk and specialty gases in 1990.

- Supervised 15 offices within 5-state region.

- Managed and supported distribution and technical service departments; 275 bulk gas customers; annual budget: $2 million.

1976 to 1983 **Chemical & Gas Products, Inc.**, Oak Brook, Illinois
Product Manager, Midwest

- Managed specialty/medical gas products/carbon dioxide with total budget $9 million. Achieved 117% of sales goals.

- Ranked in top 25% of all region salespeople for all 7 years; promoted to Regional Product Manager in 1981.

1972 to 1976 **Pennsylvania Minerals, Inc.**, Harrisburg, Pennsylvania
Sales Representative, Pennsylvania

- Managed largest sales territory ($6 million) in region. Developed USX Corporation into $2-million-dollar account.

THOMAS A. PETERSON
1643 North Laurel Lane
Village Hills, New Jersey 03303
(202) 453-5538

Job Objective: Marketing-oriented Engineering Position

WORK EXPERIENCE

August, 1982
to
Present

Aerospace Instrument Corporation of America
New Brunswick, New Jersey

World's largest producer of military flight instruments. Designs and produces CRT displays, microprocessor-based graphic generators for glass cockpits, and high-end CRT displays for industry.

Application Engineer, Marketing Department

Provide technical support and analysis of specific customer requirements. Prepare technical proposals for electronic display systems. Participated in initial systems engineering for B-65 antisubmarine warfare aircraft electronic display system. Provide extensive technical support for field sales representatives.

April, 1976
to
July, 1982

Bush-Regan & Associates
Monterey Park, New Jersey

Consulting engineers: provide studies, design, and construction supervision to municipalities, utilities, and industry.

Senior Project Manager

Managed $20-million sewer-evaluation project for Newark Metropolitan Sanitary District, which involved 26 communities, 260 engineers and technicians, and subcontractor team of 14 firms, covering 10-million feet of sanitary sewers.

Study Manager

Responsible for scoping, proposal, and management of study of sanitary sewer and combined sewer overflow for Paramus, New Jersey.

Manager of Field Operations

Managed field operations to collect all data for sewer system evaluation studies (to determine severity of clear water infiltration present in sanitary sewers). Developed new methods for computer processing of field data.

Marketing Representative

Marketed data processing and computer-aided design and drafting services to municipalities and industry. Sales: $2 million.

WORK EXPERIENCE (continued)

November, 1973
to
August, 1974

Rollerbrush Corporation
Newark, New Jersey

Project Engineer

Responsible for design, development, and testing of automated equipment and processes for production of paint roller covers.

March, 1973
to
October, 1974

Sabre Engineering
Greenway, New Jersey

Consultant

Assisted in development of automotive warning and alarm system. Responsible for fabrication and test of automobile interface simulation equipment.

October, 1963
to
October, 1973

Engineering Inspection Corporation
Greenway, New Jersey

Vice President

Marketed sewer inspection analysis services utilizing remote control camera to photograph sewer interiors. Contacted municipalities and contractors. Instrumental in development of camera and technique. Part-owner of company.

November, 1958
to
January, 1972

Delco Electronics Division, General Motors
Detroit, Michigan

Senior Project Engineer

Performed various control system engineering functions for military products.

Project Engineer

Conducted servomechanism analysis, system test and performance analysis, and system design of bombing-navigation system for aircraft.

Instructor

Taught servomechanism analysis to junior engineers.

July, 1957
to
November, 1959

Sunbeam Corporation
Livingston, New Jersey

Junior Engineer

Participated in control system engineering on several computer-indicator systems for military and commercial aircraft. Prepared proposals.

EDUCATION

Rutgers University
Bachelor of Science degree, Electrical Engineering, 1956
Elected to Phi Eta Sigma Honorary Society. Received "Sophomore Honors."

Rutgers University
27 credits toward Master's Degree in Electrical Engineering
Courses were concentrated in automatic feedback control area.

Rensselaer Polytechnic Institute
Took microprocessor courses March, 1982, to May, 1983.

PERSONAL INFORMATION

- Registered Professional Engineer, State of New Jersey.

- Computer-experienced. Fluent in FORTRAN, BASIC, Symphony, Harvard Graphics, In-A-Vision, EasyCAD, WordPerfect, and Intel 8080/8084 Assembly Language.

- Married, two adult children.

- Home owner, 25 years.

- Enjoy sailing, swimming, scuba diving, ice skating, skiing, photography, classical music, jazz, and reading.

- Sing in church choir; member of church council.

REFERENCES

- Business, educational, and personal references are available and will gladly be furnished on request.

This is an engineer's resume, and such a resume can be quite technical and deadly to read. The white space in this one, though, makes it palatable.

Never mention a specific church or denomination.

The headings on many of these sample resumes use something called small caps, which computers can do. Small caps consist of large capital letters, followed by smaller letters, which are also capitalized. This is appropriate for headlines or categories ONLY—never for the body of your resume.

If your computer or word processor can't write this way, use either capital and lowercase letters, or all caps. It helps readability to do headings and company names in boldface.

Don't ever do the entire resume in bold, however. It would be too dark and hard to read.

Current or most recent jobs deserve more space than jobs from 20 years ago. If you're 45 years old, your first job after graduation deserves only one or two lines. You don't need to tell employers everything about your life. If in doubt, leave it out. And don't repeat the same duties in one job description after another. It's boring!

DO account for all months and years on all your jobs, not just years alone, if you can. Employers are suspicious of gaps and have grown to suspect the worst when you don't account for all the months: prison, drug confinement, etc.

AMY LEE WONG
132 West Barton Avenue
Santa Rosa, California 95403-8763
(510) 555-3332

WORK EXPERIENCE

March, 1989
to
Present

Reference/Audiovisual Librarian
Santa Rosa Public Library

- Provide walk-in and phone reference service to public. Develop collections in various subject areas. Enlarged and enhanced new compact disc and video collections. Maintain extensive local history files. Conduct computer courses for public; instruct staff on use of computers.

- Qualified in operation of all new CD-ROM data retrieval systems.

January, 1988
to
July, 1989

Research Assistant
University of California - Santa Rosa

- Researched library service for people with special needs. Collected information; interviewed social service agency and library employees. Devised system and conducted data analysis with computers (resulted in report submitted and accepted by Western Shores Library System).

November, 1987
to
June, 1988

Library Assistant
American Archeological Society Library, U. of California

- Converted maps to computer format for new retrieval system.

August, 1986
to
January, 1987

Reference Librarian
Walnut Creek Public Library, Walnut Creek California

- Managed interlibrary loan requests in conjunction with reference responsibilities.

November, 1984
to
August, 1985

Library Page
Berkeley Public Library, Berkeley, California

- Searched for and shelved reading materials.

September, 1982
to
May, 1984

Peripheral Operator, Computer Science Building
University of California, Berkeley, California

- Assisted students in using microcomputers; maintained printers.

EDUCATION

1987-88	Master's Degree in Library and Information Science University of California - Berkeley
1979-84	Bachelor of Arts degree in English University of California - Santa Barbara

INTERESTS

Swimming, tennis, golf

REFERENCES

Business, personal, and educational references are readily available and will gladly be furnished on request.

JENNIFER MYERS WALTRIP
301 Mountain Avenue, Apartment #148
Santa Rosa, California 94466
(408) 555-9640

JOB OBJECTIVE: SALES REPRESENTATIVE
IN COMMUNICATIONS HARDWARE AND SERVICES

WORK EXPERIENCE

February, 1992
to
Present

> Jennifer uses quotation marks around Top Salesperson. It's a good technique! They call attention to the honor she has received in her job. For a few items in a two-pager, they're an effective tool, but don't overuse quotation marks for emphasis in a resume.

<u>Alton Electronic Communications</u>
Santa Rosa, California

<u>District Sales Representative</u>

- "Top Salesperson" for sales force, 1992, 1993.

- Sell cellular, paging, long-distance, 800-toll-free, and voice-mail services.

- Sell Novotech/Centron business products.

- Exceeded sales quota by more than 100%; exceeded #2 person's performance by 96%.

- Train new members of sales force on sales techniques and product knowledge.

- Awarded "Circle of Excellence" sales award by Novotech, 1992, 1993.

December, 1990
to
February, 1992

<u>Amalgamated Bank</u>
Rapid City, South Dakota

<u>Customer Service Representative and
Assistant Loan Officer</u>

- Successfully completed courses in "Principles of Banking" and "Statement Analysis"

- Called on new prospects and existing clients for new investment services.

WORK EXPERIENCE (continued)

Should you use page numbers in a resume? Yes. The pages may become separated or lost in the office, so don't take any chances—number each page as in these examples.

May, 1988
to
January, 1989

First State National Bank
Rapid City, South Dakota

Teller

- Worked as teller during college vacations. Performed all teller duties; handled new checking and savings accounts; sold U.S. savings bonds, American Express traveler's cheques.

EDUCATION

- Augustana College
  Sioux Falls, South Dakota
  Bachelor of Science degree
  Major: Economics
  Graduated: December, 1989

PERSONAL INFORMATION

We've all probably heard people say that personal information such as Jennifer's is nobody's business, and it has nothing to do with her qualifications. Sorry, but as you read earlier, I disagree. Companies can interview only a handful of people from thousands of applicants, and I prefer to interview the more interesting ones. Jennifer sounds like one of these, and I'd definitely invite her for an interview—any day—over people with nothing interesting to say!

Is this fair? No, but interview time is extremely valuable. A prospective employer simply can't interview more than a handful from a large pool of applicants.

- Elected President of 2,000-member Student Government at Augustana College

- Was Youth Group Leader for 10th grade church group (4 years); headed weekly meetings; counselor/planner at all retreats; planned each year's agenda

- Achieved Top Girl Scout Award at 16

- Selected for membership, Dakotaland Water Ski Team; perform various waterskiing acts, competing in local and national competitive levels

- Earned funds to pay 80% of all college expenses

- Enjoy golf, water skiing, racquetball, tennis, and classical music

REFERENCES

- Business, educational, and personal references are available and will be gladly furnished on request.

JENNIFER MYERS WALTRIP
301 Mountain Avenue, Apartment #148
Santa Rosa, California 94466
(408) 555-9640

Here she is again, in a different typeface (this one is Garamond; the first one is Times [Roman]). Which one do you like best?

JOB OBJECTIVE: SALES REPRESENTATIVE
IN COMMUNICATIONS HARDWARE AND SERVICES

WORK EXPERIENCE

February, 1992
to
Present

Alton Electronic Communications
Santa Rosa, California

District Sales Representative

- "Top Salesperson" for sales force, 1992, 1993.

- Sell cellular, paging, long-distance, 800-toll-free, and voice-mail services.

- Sell Novotech/Centron business products.

- Exceeded sales quota by more than 100%; exceeded #2 person's performance by 96%.

- Train new members of sales force on sales techniques and product knowledge.

- Awarded "Circle of Excellence" sales award by Novotech, 1992, 1993.

What about photographs on resumes? Should they be attached? No, it's not a good idea—not even if you're great-looking. There's too much potential for trouble if you do include them: equal opportunity hiring laws, class action lawsuits, etc., so leave the photos out. The exception: actors, models, and other similar jobs often require photos of several professionally photographed poses, showing several different "looks" to demonstrate versatility. (Some companies will return your resume to you—unread—if you do send a photo, asking you to "please send this without a photograph .")

December, 1990
to
February, 1992

Amalgamated Bank
Rapid City, South Dakota

Customer Service Representative and
Assistant Loan Officer

- Successfully completed courses in "Principles of Banking" and "Statement Analysis"

- Called on new prospects and existing clients for new investment services.

WORK EXPERIENCE (continued)

May, 1988
to
January, 1989

First State National Bank
Rapid City, South Dakota

Teller

- Worked as teller during college vacations. Performed all teller duties; handled new checking and savings accounts; sold U.S. savings bonds, American Express traveler's cheques.

EDUCATION

- Augustana College
  Sioux Falls, South Dakota
  Bachelor of Science degree
  Major: Economics
  Graduated: December, 1989

PERSONAL INFORMATION

- Elected President of 2,000-member Student Government at Augustana College

- Was Youth Group Leader for 10th grade church group (4 years); headed weekly meetings; counselor/planner at all retreats; planned each year's agenda

- Achieved Top Girl Scout Award at 16

- Selected for membership, Dakotaland Water Ski Team; perform various waterskiing acts, competing in local and national competitive levels

- Earned funds to pay 80% of all college expenses

- Enjoy golf, water skiing, racquetball, tennis, and classical music

REFERENCES

- Business, educational, and personal references are available and will be gladly furnished on request.

KIM R. KRAHN
3579 South High Point Road
Charlotte, North Carolina 28210
(412) 555-6199

WORK EXPERIENCE

January, 1990
to
Present

Executive Suites & Business Offices
Charlotte, North Carolina

Executive Receptionist

- Receptionist/telephone receptionist for 25 companies and organizations in executive-suites complex. Responsible for 60 incoming lines; handle average of 30 to 35 calls hourly. Greet, host, and direct incoming visitors and guests for executive clients.

- Perform general office duties, including: typing of letters, labels, envelopes; invoicing clients for monthly charges; liaison with overnight air-shipping firms. Typing speed: 55 words per minute. Compensation: hourly wage, overtime; no fringe benefits.

June, 1987
to
December, 1989

Sears, Roebuck & Company
Charlotte, North Carolina

Interior Decorator/Design Consultant

- Performed on-site and in-store consultation for retail/individual and business customers regarding designing, decorating, colorizing, and furnishing of homes and offices. Won sales awards for meeting and exceeding assigned quotas. Method of compensation: commission sales.

EDUCATION

- Graduate, Interior Design Program, Class of 1988, Central Piedmont Community College

- Graduate, North Charlotte High School, Class of 1987

> Kim has office experience but went to interior design school. Should she state a job objective at the top so that people know what she prefers? Not necessarily. It's optional. When you're young, people "forgive" you for trying this and that. But once you reach 30 or 35, your resume and career should be more focused; you shouldn't be bouncing around from job to job, changing fields dramatically and often. Job hopping may be excusable when you're under 30, but watch out after that! If you've established a "two years here, three years there" kind of track record, you do NOT want that pattern to develop into a lifelong, unbreakable habit.

PERSONAL INFORMATION

Fast-food experience: is it relevant? It may not be directly related, and you may not think it's helpful, but employers like it! The coordination required and the constant public contact make for good background. Also, they know it doesn't pay a great deal of money, and your job at Wendy's, McDonald's, or Burger King shows that you're willing to do some "grunt work."

- Honor Student in high school business, bookkeeping, and typing courses. Courses included accounting and computer operations.

- Member, high school choir; participated in athletics.

- Paid 100% of college tuition and expenses by working at Hardee's (fast food) restaurant from May, 1986, to June, 1987 (as high school student). Selected as Crew Leader; supervised eight employees.

- Member, Carolina Interiors Association while student at Central Piedmont Community College.

- Enjoy aerobics, walking, outdoor recreation; do craft work and read extensively as hobbies.

REFERENCES

- Business and personal references are available and will gladly be furnished on request.

MICHAEL ALLAN FORDHAM

226 Manchester Street
Manchester, New Hampshire 03103
Telephone: (603) 555-2244

Here's a nice one-pager: a good blend of jobs, activities, offices, grades, — everything.

CAREER OBJECTIVE
Systems Analyst/Programmer

EDUCATION

Bachelor of Science degree in Business, with honors: "Cum Laude"
New Hampshire College, Manchester, New Hampshire
Degree granted May, 1994; 3.59/4.0 grade average
Major: Management Information Systems

WORK EXPERIENCE

June, 1994
to
December, 1994

Royale Toiletries & Cosmetics Distributing Company
Cincinnati, Ohio

Field Advertising Representative

Administer national field force of 150 people. Design and implement national computerized reporting system for field advertising representatives. Coordinate training at corporate headquarters for all field reps.

September, 1992
to
May, 1994

Computer Systems Technology Corporation
Manchester, New Hampshire

Programmer Analyst

Responsible for analyzing needs, systems design, programming, testing, documenting, and user training. Worked with DOS JCL, VSAM and TOTAL Database. Environment: 4341 & 4381. IBM PC with Lotus 1-2-3. Languages: BASIC, ANS COBOL, FORTRAN, RPG II.

HONORS AND ACHIEVEMENTS

- Won "Student Affairs Award" for outstanding contributions to the New Hampshire College community; represented college at various national conventions; Senior Class President.

- Chairman, fund-raising pageant for underprivileged children.

- Honor Roll all four years in high school; selected for Boys' State.

- Active in church youth group; pastor's assistant three years.

- Won scholarship all four years in college; worked to earn tuition and expense money and paid 75% of college costs.

REFERENCES

- Business, personal and school references gladly furnished on request.

PETER J. HILSBERG
1948 Sound View Drive
Seattle, Washington 98112-3457

(206) 555-6266

EXPERIENCE

Northwest Coca Cola Bottling Co.   Seattle, Washington
March, 1992, to July, 1994

District Juice Manager. Position created to introduce Minute Maid Fruit Juices, Fruitopia, and Nestea Iced Tea in market. Sold products directly to grocery, convenience, and other retail stores throughout Seattle-Tacoma metro area.

Corporate Parts Manager. Responsible for purchasing, inventory, and distribution of (cold drink dispenser) equipment parts for all Washington State Divisions. Scheduled new installations of cold drink equipment. Promoted to this position in October, 1993.

Fountain Sales Representative. Territory manager for sales of fountain syrup in Seattle metro and adjacent counties. Responsibilities: Direct sales of fountain equipment and fountain syrup to taverns, restaurants, and night clubs. Sold promotional material to increase retail sales, merchandising, and customer maintenance. Also: Special events and route sales. Exceeded sales quotas each quarter. Converted four major accounts from competitive products.

Beer & Beverage Brands   Seattle, Washington
March, 1988, to October, 1991

Special Events Coordinator. Set up special events sponsored by National Brewing company and National Brands: exhibits and events at Seattle Seafair, Washington State Fair, Taste of Seattle Days, church festivals, and other events. Duties: merchandising, route sales, and direct sales. Route sales in winter holiday season.

Inner-State Distributing   Spokane, Washington
January, 1991, to May, 1991

Campus Representative. Initiated campus "sales and promotion internship" program to increase sales of National Beer products. Set-up and promoted National Brands events for campus organizations.

Banner Vendors & Concessions   Seattle, Washington
June, 1982, to Present (summers only)

Beverage Manager. National Brands at Seattle Seafair (5 years); National Brands Pavilion at Washington State Fair (4 years).

EDUCATION

Bachelor of Arts Degree in Journalism/Advertising, May, 1989
University of Washington, Seattle, Washington
Major: Journalism/Advertising; Minor: Psychology

HONORS AND ACTIVITIES

- Member, Phi Gamma Delta Fraternity
- Student Director, national ad campaign, Kellogg Co.
- Attained Eagle Scout Award, 1982
- "Fountain Salesman of Quarter": December, 1990; March, 1991
- Promoted to District Juice Manager, May, 1992

REFERENCES

Business and personal references gladly furnished on request.

Barbara Jane Roberts
8213 Rolling Avenue
Richmond, Virginia 23217-3371
(804) 555-7147

Position in Educational Sales and Marketing/Admissions

Work Experience

Currently:

Virginia College of Business
Richmond, Virginia

Director of Admissions

- Responsible for all marketing, sales, and admissions functions. Develop and implement all advertising programs in various media (radio, TV, newspaper, etc.). VCB is a 1000-student, college-level, nonprofit institution. Supervise 16 admissions representatives, including four outside sales reps.

- Areas of responsibility include admissions testing, financial aid, and securing government grants. Represent school at community activities and meetings and at various public functions. Extensive public speaking.

- Teach adult students: sales, marketing, travel and tourism, mathematics, history, advertising.

> I can hear you now: "Three pages? Isn't that too long?"
>
> Not really. You grab the reader's attention with a wide-open look on the first page, and once he or she begins to read your easy-to-read results and accomplishments (quantified, of course), the person actually never notices whether the rest of the resume is two pages or three.

Five Years

Central College of Business
Omaha, Nebraska

Department Chair, Travel and Tourism Studies

- Responsible for 200-student annual enrollment. Develop and update all course curricula. Supervise faculty and staff of six. Placed 100% of graduates.

- Maintain strict criteria for school and program accreditation by national and international accrediting bodies.

- Instruct classes for adult students entering travel industry: sales, marketing, destination geography, ticketing, advertising, public relations business writing.

- Train instructors and staff for other school curricula on request of school director.

> This applicant had some gaps in her work history—nothing serious—but she covers them by writing "five years," "seven years," etc. What do you think of this idea? It might be worth a try if you have gaps to cover.

Five Years

Complete Travel Agencies, Inc.
Omaha, Nebraska

President

- Created, developed, and sold wholesale tour packages for Australia, New Zealand and the South Pacific, the Middle East, and Israel. Selected as authorized QANTAS wholesaler; became largest Midwest tour packager for QANTAS. Won two tourism awards from State of Israel.

Seven Years

Las Vegas Charter Tour Operators, Inc.
Omaha, Nebraska

Director, Sales and Marketing

- Developed and coordinated all sales and marketing activities for one of nation's largest wholesalers of domestic tour packages.

- Built volume of room nights in Las Vegas from zero to 560,000 in five-year period.

Six Years

Central Travel Agencies
Omaha, Nebraska

Division Vice-President and General Manager

- Expanded company from one retail office to seven; built staff from three to 37 people. Hired, trained, and selected personnel. Directly supervised seven managers. Reported directly to corporate executive vice-president.

- Developed gross annual volume of $10 million dollars.

Four Years

Northwest Airlines, Inc.
Atlanta, Georgia

Passenger Sales Agent

Personal Information

- Married to John Roberts, professional engineer; 1 daughter

- Active in church work; church school teacher

- Wrote numerous articles, books, pamphlets

- Awarded "Educator of the Year," Central College, 1990

- Bachelor's Degree from University of Nebraska; degree awarded, 1959

- Master's Degree candidate at Nova University; degree to be awarded in 1996

- Instructor, Richmond Area Vocational-Technical College, 1987-present

References

- Business, personal, and educational references are available and will be furnished on request.

STEVE A. JORRIS
6755 North Malone Parkway
Whitesails, Wisconsin 53218-6683
(414) 555-4950

Job Objective: A Position in **Quality Assurance Management**
with a Manufacturing Firm

EMPLOYMENT HISTORY

August, 1985
to
Present

Electro-ped, Incorporated
Milwaukee, Wisconsin

Assistant Supervisor, Quality Systems
(since July, 1992)

- Supervise 185 employees, 25 directly, in electronics and control panel departments of manufacturer of equipment for the beverage packing industry.

- Implemented and supervised new calibration system; saved $10,000+ within first 7 months.

- Designed and implemented 5 custom packaging methods, which reduced damage costs by 75%.

- Developed and implemented international-repair-and-return system to guarantee product return to customers within 13 days of initial failure.

- Supervise reformatting of manufacturing standards for soldering (hole & SMD technology), hardware, component insertion, and wire wrapping.

Assistant Supervisor of Field Service Returns
(since December, 1991)

- Developed new inventory tracking system that decreased late orders from 40 orders to 1 per month.

- Implemented new customer inquiry program that saved $30,000 within first three months of operation.

- Developed and supervised new mandatory callback contact program for customers.

Warning: This book is no doubt the only resume book **anywhere** that has the following much-too-long example.

But it served its purpose well.

It was sent in response to an employer's direct request: "You've been recommended to us. Would you please send a resume as soon as you can?"

So Steve **knew** that he wasn't in competition with 200 other candidates' resumes. He knew it would be read because he was the only person the company was considering at the time.

Steve sent them his entire "sales packet" including: cover letter – one page; resume – three pages; reference list – one page; seminars and training – one page; and "testimonials"– one page. Seven pages in all!

EMPLOYMENT HISTORY (continued)

Assistant Supervisor, Quality Control
(since March, 1988)

- Designed and implemented new quality improvement notification system to solicit and use employee input.

- Improved MTBF (Mean Time Between Failures) program to inform design engineers of reliability problems by designing product return tracking system.

- Implemented supplier efficiency program, which eliminated three vendors unable to meet standards.

Quality Control Technician (since January, 1987)

- Enhanced labor-intensive work center to new process-controlled operation; 50% reduction in processing time and 50% improvement in product-line reliability.

- Assisted in developing failure-coding system that eliminated 80 hours of post-assembly inspection/wk.

- Designed rework monitoring system on incentive basis; reduced rework from 5% of direct labor hours to .2% weekly.

Electronics Technician (since May, 1986)

- Troubleshooter and repair person for printed circuit board assemblies, using diagnostic equipment. Calibrated mechanical test equipment.

Electronics Assembler (since August, 1985)
- Prepared electronic components; assembled printed circuit boards; operated wave soldering machine. Manufactured PCB assemblies; performed inspections.

PERSONAL INFORMATION

- Worked as retail salesperson/manager at K-Mart: September, 1983, to September, 1985; ordered/maintained inventory for 7 departments.

- Worked as custom cabinet fabricator at Fine Line Design, Inc. from January, 1981, to July, 1983; built and installed cabinets.

- Born December 8, 1965; 5' 11" tall, 170 lbs.; excellent health.

- Member:
  - American Society for Quality Control
  - Milwaukee Quality Improvement Network
  - Milwaukee Area Technical College Alumni Association
  - International Physical Fitness Association

- Honors:
  - "Most Influential Speech & Personal Development" Award in Dale Carnegie Management Course, 1992
  - "Human Relations" Award for most convincing speech on self-improvement, 1990
  - "Employee of the Month," K-Mart, April, 1985
  - "Top Sales Producer for electronics and appliance department for 6 months, K-Mart, 1984-85

- Hobbies: Business reading, investments, sports, restoring old cars, woodworking, traveling, camping, coaching boys' soccer

EDUCATION

- Bachelor of Science degree
  Ottawa University
  Graduated May, 1994; 3.75/4.0 grade average; honor student

- Associate Degree in Supervisory Management
  Milwaukee Area Technical College
  Graduated December, 1992; 3.55/4.0 grade average; honor student

REFERENCES

- Enclosed on separate list; each person has given permission to be contacted.

REFERENCES
for
Steve A. Jorris

Harold J. Remley
H. J. Remley & Associates
6410 Enterprise Lane, Suite 200
Milwaukee, Wisconsin 53209
(414) 271-3121

University of Wisconsin Professor
Author of 3 books
Have known Prof. Remley for 6 years

David Swanson
Career Seminars
1033 N. Mayfair Road, Suite 200
Milwaukee, Wisconsin 53226
(414) 259-0265

Career and Marketing Consultant
Public Speaker, Author
Have known Dave for 2 years

Herbert T. Howard, President
Financial Services, Inc.
7700 Oriole Road
Milwaukee, Wisconsin 53721
(414) 555-7789

Certified Financial Planner
Have known Mr. Howard for 2 years

Terry Solomon
Dale Carnegie Courses
802 West Broadway
Milwaukee, Wisconsin 53203
(414) 555-5960

Area Manager for Dale Carnegie Courses
Experienced instructor, trainer, consultant
Have known Terry for 2 years

NOTE: Additional business, personal, and educational references are readily available and will be furnished on request.

Seminars Attended

an Addendum to the Resume of

Steve A. Jorris

- "Effective Technical Writing"   National Seminars Group

- "Implementing ISO 9000/Q90
  in Small- /Medium-sized Companies"   UW College of Engineering

- "Supplier Certification"   Purchasing Management Group

- "The Dale Carnegie Course"   Dale Carnegie Courses

- "Human Relations & Effective Speaking"   Dale Carnegie Courses

- "The Supervisor's Job Today"   Management Education Council

- "Self Esteem & Peak Performance"   CareerTrack

- "Quality Circle Leader Training"   Electro-ped, Inc.

- "Supervisory Management"   Electro-ped, Inc.

- "Supervision"   Zenger-Miller

- "Just In Time Manufacturing"   Harry Remley & Associates

- "Train the Trainer"   Electro-ped, Inc.

- "Equal Employment Opportunity"   EEOC/Electro-ped, Inc.

Typical Quotes and Comments

for

Steve Jorris

"Steve is respectful, responsive, helpful, flexible, directive and more!!"
Kelly Sommers, Electro-ped, Inc.

"I am proud to work under Steve's leadership."
Chung Chang-Wei, Electro-ped, Inc.

"In the two years I have worked for Steve, I have observed his outstanding performance. Not only is Steve punctual in responding to problems, but he gives one his undivided attention. He may work too hard!! He is always, always on hand to help. He is by far one of the finest supervisors I have ever had."
Catherine Walters, Electro-ped, Inc.

"Steve Jorris is one of the truly bright lights among the management people I know. He is mature beyond his years; he seems to know what to do in any situation. He is bright, well-groomed, intellectually sound, energetic and enthusiastic, and he possesses rare abilities in dealing with his people . . . or dealing with anyone."

David Swanson, President, Career Seminars

"Steve is very talented and capable . . . lives by the highest standards of values and ethical behavior . . . bright, dedicated and has a great affinity for knowledge . . . presents himself in a highly professional manner and is very pleasant to work with, even on the tough stages of a project."

Harold J. Remley, Ph.D.

405 North Malone Parkway
Whitesails, Wisconsin 53530

February 16, 1994

Mr. James Polano
Manager, Quality and Organizational Development
Warren Electronics, Inc.
4465 Corollary Avenue
Sheboygan, Wisconsin 53082-3342

Dear Mr. Polano:

Thank you for your call and kind words about my background and experience. I am pleased that Dr. Harry Remley recommended me to you. As you suggested, I am forwarding the enclosed material about my background.

Dr. Remley has spoken highly of your firm. I have been impressed with the rapid growth and exceptional quality of product for which Warren Electronics, Inc., has become well-known.

I will take the liberty of calling your office in a week or so to see if we might meet to discuss the possibility of meeting each other for lunch or a short discussion. My home phone number is 414-555-3339; my work is number is 414-555-7322, in case you prefer to contact me before I call you.

Sincerely,

Steve Jorris

Steve A. Jorris

Is Steve's resume too long? Is it "just too much?" No, probably not for this specific situation.

They liked his seven-page packet, and they liked him. They brought him in for an interview, lunch, a tour, etc. After two more interviews, he got a significant offer from "Warren Electronics" at a nice-sized salary increase!

This long windedness may not be for you, but on some occasions it does the job.

In the educational field, for example, where resumes are usually called "Curriculum Vitæ" (which means something like "an itemization of your life"), the extra length of a resume usually makes the candidate more impressive than if he or she has only a page or two.

Because most resumes are for business use, however, we recommend that you stick to one, two, or (if you absolutely must) three pages. All of them should be wide-open, wide-margin, very easy-to-read pages.

RESUME WORKSHEET

Instructions. Complete each section as you want this information to appear on your resume itself. Be complete. Do not use abbreviations unless necessary. Be brief. Emphasize your accomplishments and skills that are directly related to the job you want. And use a pencil to allow you to make changes later.

Many people find it helpful to write out a draft version of the more complicated sections on other sheets of paper first. *Then* go ahead and complete this worksheet. Use additional pages as needed so that what you write on the worksheet here is very close to what you want to put on your resume.

Identification

Full name: _____

Address: _____

City: _____

State or province: _____

ZIP or postal code: _____

Phone numbers. List these as they will appear on your resume. Include your area code within parentheses. The optional comment lines are for brief comments, such as "home #," "office #," "leave message," or whatever.

Primary phone number: (_____) _____ - _____

Comment: _____

Alternative phone number: (_____) _____ - _____

Comment: _____

Education & Training

Begin with your most recent education or training. If you have attended many schools, condense these into a manageable number. Look for the best way to display your educational experiences; usually, that will be a listing of the *one or two* schools where you did the work that led directly into the career you are in. Or the programs where you received your most important, or most impressive-sounding, training.

(Give the month and year you graduated, or the class in which you were enrolled, such as "Class of 1989"; "June, 1988"; "Graduation: December, 1990"; etc.)

SCHOOL NAME: _____

City and state or province: _____

Class: _____

RESUME WORKSHEET
Education & Training (continued)

List degree, certificate, or diploma received: _____

Major: _____

Minor(s): _____

Overall grade point average or class standing: _____

Grade point average in subjects related to job: _____

Related activities and accomplishments: _____

_____

_____

_____

_____

SCHOOL NAME: _____

City and state or province: _____

Class: _____

List degree, certificate, or diploma received: _____

_____

Major: _____

Minor(s): _____

Overall grade point average or class standing: _____

Grade point average in subjects related to job: _____

Related activities and accomplishments: _____

_____

_____

_____

_____

SCHOOL NAME: _____

City and state or province: _____

Class: _____

RESUME WORKSHEET
Education & Training (continued)

List degree, certificate, or diploma received: _____

Major: _____

Minor(s): _____

Overall grade point average or class standing: _____

Grade point average in subjects related to job: _____

Related activities and accomplishments: _____

_____

_____

_____

Experience

Begin with your most recent full-time work experiences and work back in time. Devote more space to recent jobs or jobs that are more relevant to support the job you want now.

CURRENT OR MOST RECENT JOB _____

Name of organization: _____

City and state or province: _____

Date you started working there: _____
(Month and year only, with name of month spelled out)

Date you ended your employment there: _____

(Resumes often state "Present," as in "June, 1986, to Present," even though you no longer are working there. This is not considered untruthful by most, but you can also list the month you left. It is no longer considered unusual to be unemployed and seeking employment for several months; it's normal.)

Job title: _____

_____

(If you held several job titles at one organization, please see the resume examples for several good ideas for making this situation understandable.)

Job description. Tell what you did, as clearly and exactly as you can. Emphasize *results* and *accomplishments* directly attributable to the fact that you were there. Whenever possible, use numbers, percentages, increases, and dollar figures to indicate some *exactness* in what you accomplished while there.

RESUME WORKSHEET
Work Experience (continued)

_____

_____

_____

_____

NEXT JOB _____

Name of organization: _____

City and state or province: _____

Date you started working: _____

Date you ended your employment: _____

Job title: _____

_____

(If you held several job titles at one organization, please see the resume examples for several good ideas for making this situation understandable.)

Job description. Unless this job is important in supporting your current job objective, be briefer with its description. Eliminate repetitions. List only important results and accomplishments, duties or responsibilities.

_____

_____

_____

_____

NEXT JOB _____

Name of organization: _____

City and state or province: _____

Date you started working: _____

Date you ended your employment: _____

Job title: _____

_____

Job description. Unless this job is important in supporting your current job objective, be even briefer here. If you can hold it down to a few phrases, even to two phrases or three, that would be fine. Try it.

_____

_____

_____

_____

NEXT JOB _____

Name of organization: _____

City and state or province: _____

Date you started working: _____

Date you ended your employment: _____

Job title: _____

_____

Job description. If you have more than four previous jobs, consider simple listings here—or combine all of those "miscellaneous" jobs into one statement like "held various positions while going to school."

_____

_____

_____

_____

Honors, Awards, and Achievements

What non-school-related organizations did you join? Church group? 4-H? Job's Daughters? Key Club? Volunteers? ROTC? Political campaigns? Musical groups? Nonschool sports? Coaching? Tutoring?

Name of organization: _____

My role: _____

_____

_____

RESUME WORKSHEET
Personal Information

Include any special skills, attributes, hobbies, or other information that supports your job objective but doesn't fit elsewhere.

_____

_____

_____

_____

_____

WHAT OTHERS SAY

If you choose to include testimonials in your resume, put here the statements you want to include.

_____

_____

_____

_____

_____

_____

_____

_____

_____

_____

_____

References

You do not need to include references on your resume. If space permits, you can add an optional statement, such as one of the following:

> *Business and personal references are available and will be furnished on request.*   or
>
> *Excellent business and personal references are available.*   or
>
> *Complete business and personal references are available and will gladly be furnished on request.*

Congratulations! Now you are ready to put together your resume's final draft. Before you begin, take a look at the *common resume mistakes* on the next page to make sure you are on the right track.

Common Resume Mistakes Checklist

✓ Is the resume too wordy? Have I edited statements down to a few words, powerful words, short words?

✓ Is the layout attractive and *open,* with enough white space?

✓ Is my Job Objective specific? Short enough?

✓ Have I checked the spelling of difficult words?

✓ Are my job-description phrases action-oriented? Have I included *results* and *accomplishments?* Have I used *numbers* and *percentages* wherever possible to show real results?

✓ Have I given too much information (such as company address, phone number, supervisor's name, titles, ZIP codes, and so on)?

✓ Does the layout I'm planning to use *flow?* Or does it *jerk* and dart from one part of the page to another?

✓ Does the information sound like I am bragging about myself, rather than presenting hard facts and undoctored information?

✓ Have I correctly removed all proper names that show a political, religious, or philosophical preference?

✓ Have I listed a proper number of schools, rather than too many?

✓ Have I compressed my old jobs into a small space, instead of telling about them in detail?

✓ Have I listed too many part-time jobs separately, instead of more appropriately grouping them together?

✓ Have I given too much information, expecting the reader to pick out what is most important, instead of editing down to a suitable length?

✓ Have I kept the length down to two pages—or in the most extreme case to three pages—including sufficient white space on each page?

✓ Have I converted highly technical language into easy-to-understand and easy-to-read words, based on the person who will be reading and reviewing this document?

Now, check the following elements that give your resume readability.

Test for Readability

✓ Upper- and lowercase letters, not all-capital letters

✓ Serif type face

✓ Use of bullets where appropriate (periods, followed by 3-4 spaces, followed by an item or phrase)

✓ Adequate leading, or spacing, between lines or items or job descriptions or sections

✓ Plenty of white space for a clean look

✓ Wide margins (1 inch on each side, and at top and bottom)

✓ No hyphenated words, no split phrases

✓ Indentations consistent and used where necessary for clarity

✓ Proper names of more than one word kept on the same line

✓ Columnar format for body of resume, with maximum width of 3½ to 4½ inches

✓ Short paragraphs

✓ Short words

✓ Phrases, not sentences

✓ Phrases that begin with action verbs

✓ Short phrases or sentences, if necessary, throughout

✓ Upper-left to upper-right *flow*

✓ Few or no abbreviations, and very careful use of them

▶ You're on Your Way

If you've followed the hints given here, you're well on your way to having a resume that will be not only read but also admired.

People who will be reading, and screening, your resume may or may not be resume experts themselves. In fact, they may know little about resumes. They may even be reading groups of resumes for the first time.

But even those who are new at the job *know what they like to read.* If you've followed my advice so far, that's what you're giving them.

In the next chapter, you learn about another important element of the job search: *letters.* They're more important than most job seekers think.

Writing resumes isn't exactly fun for most of us. And when we're done, we don't look forward to writing a letter to accompany the resume. We'd rather *not* write for a while.

But sometimes the cover letter is even *more* important than the resume itself. The next chapter tells you why.

Chapter 7
The Cover Letter

The Cover Letter Is Your Introduction

The cover letter accompanies a resume and is its proper "companion."

The resume might be thought of as "needing an introduction." You may do this introduction yourself, in person. Or someone else, perhaps a friend who works at the organization, may do it for you. Or the cover letter can serve as your "introduction."

But you *do* need an introduction. Don't just attempt to "barge your way in."

Cover letters provide an opportunity to deliver a more personalized message to the recipient; the resume itself is usually produced in quantity— 25, 50, 100 or so—and there is little chance to customize each one for individual employers.

But the cover letter provides the perfect place to do this customizing, to make the communication a personal one between employer and applicant.

Your cover letter should always be typed, on a very fine quality office-type typewriter...or on a letter-quality or laser printer.

It would be foolish to prepare a first-quality resume and then include with it a cover letter typed on an old portable home typewriter...or on a dot-matrix computer printer.

Do it right! Doing it right also means that you *never* mass-produce a cover letter. Cover letters are individually prepared, individually written, individually typed or printed, and the material in it should be aimed directly at the target...the market...the recipient.

Cover letters which begin "To Whom It May Concern:" or "Good Morning," or "Dear Sir or Madam:" are as incorrect as an uninvited guest at a formal party.

Impersonal letters don't often receive a warm reception from employers. The nonpersonalized cover letter may, indeed, be treated the same way you probably treat mass-produced advertising materials in the mail. In the old days, this was called "junk mail." Now we're urged to call it direct marketing.

Many folks throw junk mail right into the wastebasket!

▶ Don't Send Cover Letters to Strangers

Because a cover letter is a form of personal correspondence, you should use the name of the person who will receive the letter. Learn the person's name, and then spell it correctly.

If you are using the cover letter as a follow-up after a meeting or phone conversation in which you promised to send a resume, be *certain* to spell everything correctly. It's bad enough if someone receives a misspelled letter from someone he or she doesn't know, but to receive a letter with an incorrectly spelled name or title or company from someone he or she *does* know might spell disaster for you.

Resumes are usually produced in quantities, so the employer may not expect an individually tailored resume. Cover letters, however, provide an excellent opportunity to be more personal than a resume allows, or is *supposed* to be, and to highlight anything on a resume that might be important to the employer, but is "buried" in your resume. Here are some advantages of a good cover letter:

1. You can focus it *directly* toward a specific job without redoing or customizing the entire resume.
2. You can highlight in the cover letter one or two things from the resume.
3. You can include things important to a specific job, but which are not included in the resume.
4. Headlines are the most widely read part of a newspaper, and, similarly, cover letters are often read more carefully than resumes.
5. You can use elegant stationery for cover letters.
6. Cover letters take less time to compose than resumes.

The Golden Rule for Job Hunters

The Golden Rule for job hunters has been around forever. Career counselors praise its merits to each client. But job hunters often fail to heed its wisdom. They go merrily along their way, wasting valuable time and money by choosing not to follow it. The Golden Rule says this:

Always use your contacts. If you don't have the right contact for a specific situation, do what you must to create the right contact.

It's the same in business as it's always been. It's *who you know,* and especially *whom you will take the trouble to meet from now on,* that will make the difference between success and failure in getting hired.

Go through the back door of a company, not the front. By this, we mean that you should cultivate the acquaintanceship or friendship of someone who works there, so that you don't have to walk in the front door and talk to the receptionist like a stranger. Instead, get to know someone who works in the organization. When you have established a relationship with an employee, you may feel free to ask for an introduction to someone in the department in which you hope to work.

If you take the time and trouble to get to know someone in the organization, you gain a *tremendous* advantage!

Do not break this Golden Rule! When you know someone personally, and especially when a relationship has been established, your letters stand a much improved chance of being read. Letters from strangers rarely receive the same attention as letters from friends.

Phone calls or letters from *friends,* or from *friends of friends,* get attention!

Would *you* ever turn away the friend of a respected friend or business colleague who came to you for advice or help?

Of course not. And neither will potential employers.

How do you do this? Here are a few ideas:

1. Ministers, priests, and rabbis know many people from their congregations and parishes.

2. People from organizations tend to eat lunch in restaurants close to work.

3. People from organizations often socialize after work in certain nearby establishments.

4. Meetings of professional organizations and chapters bring together people from dozens, scores, and even hundreds of organizations. Their meetings are often open to guests, prospective members, or people who merely drop in to hear the speaker.

5. College and university career development offices keep extensive files on local companies and often include names and phone numbers of employees.

6. College and university alumni offices have the names of alumni with addresses, phone numbers, their employers, and position held, and often include business addresses and phone numbers as well.

7. Find a copy of the directory from your last high school reunion—whether you attended the reunion or not.

8. Find copies of directories from classes behind or ahead of yours. These include people you may have known or whom your siblings may know.

9. Have the right *attitude* about getting to know people! That attitude is "I can get to know almost anyone, in any organization, if I *think* I can."

10. Friendships and acquaintanceships are a two-way street and a long-term situation. Expect to give as many favors, or many more, than you are asking for, and don't forget the kindness of people who do you favors.

The Network Advantage

Your *network* consists of all the people you know—and have known—plus all the people they know. So with a telephone call, or after two or three calls, you can tie into a vast *network*.

You may have seen the TV commercials claiming that "anyone in the world is accessible to you within six phone calls." Such a seemingly outrageous claim isn't as farfetched as you might think. I, for one, believe it.

For job hunters, this personal network of *people you know* and *people they know* is **very** important.

So, what if you don't know *anyone* in the organization in which you would like to work?

Use your *network!* Use the names of people you know, and names of people *they* know, to get the name of someone who works in the organization you're targeting or in the field you hope to enter.

But what if you think *no one* in your network of contacts knows anyone in the organization or your chosen field? Should you conclude that you're "out in the cold" and must go in "cold" by the front door?

NO! Don't give up so quickly.

Use the ideas above or come up with your own. Through your network, you can *always* locate the name of someone in the organization, or who is doing what you want to do, or who is working in the field you've chosen.

Keep on looking! It may take a few extra hours or a few more phone calls. (Some of these may be long distance calls, so be prepared for a little extra expense—it's well worth it!)

If you persist, you *will* find the contact you need.

▶ Tips on Writing a Good Cover Letter

Write to a Person, Not to a Title

This is the #1 most important tip. Use your network to get the name you need; then **use it!** In your opening paragraph, name the person who referred you to the person you are now writing.

A colleague of mine, a successful executive recruiter on the East Coast, receives thousands of unsolicited (and unwanted!) resumes annually. Which ones does he read? Which ones receive a reply? ***Only those that use the name of someone the recruiter knows personally.*** He treats the others as "junk mail" but replies to anyone who uses the name of someone he knows. After all, it is only good manners to respond to a "friend of a friend."

Address your cover letter, if at all possible, to the person who has the power to hire you. This is probably the person who manages the department you want to work in.

Be aware that the person who does the hiring is usually *not* the personnel director, human resources manager, interviewer, or screener. Most of these people have the power to screen you *out,* but few have the actual power to hire.

Use a Strong Opening Statement

Start the letter by using a referral name if possible: "Bob Perry, your former executive vice-president, suggested I write you. He felt that we might have some mutual benefits to discuss and feels very positive toward your organization."

If, after trying everything we recommend to you, you do *not* have a referral name, open with a strong positive statement. Start with your *best* selling point. Shortly thereafter, name the position you are applying for, or very specifically explain what you hope to do, or mention the department you're targeting. Here are some examples of good opening lines to give you some ideas for creating your own:

> *I recently graduated from Paramount Business College with a 3.75 grade average and received my Associate Degree in Secretarial Science and Office Management.*

> *Enclosed is my resume for your advertised position of Assistant Cook.*

> *I recently graduated from Johnson County Community College with a Diploma in Food Service and have worked successfully as a cook for Bob's Big Boy on Wallace Avenue for the past two years.*

> *Your advertisement in* The Tribune *for a Computer Programmer matches my qualifications exactly.*

> *I have two years of experience as an Operator/Programmer with L. G. Williams, Inc., and have now received my Certificate in Data Processing.*

> *After five years of successful experience in a similar position in Portland, I am enclosing my application for the Community Development Officer position.*

> *This sounds like the job I have been waiting for! It appears to match the qualifications gained in my seven years of social work experience.*

A good opening statement grabs attention without turning off the reader. It helps to "categorize" your application if the organization is advertising several openings.

If you do not have a very *specific* opening line in your cover letter, your resume might end up in the wrong place or in the wrong hands. Or it could take a long time to reach the right person as it floats through the various departments of a large organization.

Each person who receives your resume (by mistake!) will send it on to someone else (who may also be uninterested in it or may be the wrong person to be receiving it!).

Sometimes, someone along the line will "file it." If this happens, you're "dead in the water," and you will probably never hear from anyone in that organization again.

Or they may destroy your resume or toss it away, deciding not to route it further. And you're dead again!

So you must do whatever you can to keep your resume alive, and to get it onto the desk of someone who has the power to hire a person like you.

Keep Your Letter Short, Make It Look Good, and Include Key Strengths

How long should a cover letter be? Keep it on *one page*. And the body of your cover letter should occupy *no more* than about 50 percent of the page.

Use plenty of white space. Keep your sentences short, make your paragraphs short, and design your letter so that it looks inviting and easy to read. If you do not, it may not be read at all!

Write several drafts! Edit your letter as carefully as you do your resume. It must be perfect!

It should be tailored as closely as you know how to the recipient's needs and requirements, as best you know them.

To do this, highlight from your background the best items that directly qualify you for the job. Bring out your strong points...the things someone might miss in the resume itself.

Your objective is to arouse the reader's interest immediately, with something directly related, very *interesting*...and very attractively presented in an easy-to-read format.

Signing Your Cover Letter

When signing your typewritten cover letter, type your *real* name. If you want, sign your nickname, or the name by which you like to be called. But type your first and last names. (Skip your middle initial; using it can sound a bit arrogant.)

If your name is Paul Charleston Bosworth Jr., and if they call you "Chuck," and if your formal written name is P. Charleston Bosworth, type Charleston Bosworth; then sign it "Chuck Bosworth." If you are known as Charles, sign it that way.

▶ Sample Cover Letters

Most cover letters follow a standard outline:

- The first paragraph states your strongest point(s) and the job for which you want to be considered.
- The second paragraph states why you want to work for this organization (talk about them, not about yourself!).
- The third paragraph highlights skills and qualifications from your resume that are relevant to that particular organization.
- The fourth paragraph requests an interview and suggests how you will follow up.

Here are five examples of good cover letters.

4550 Parrier Street
Espinosa, California 98866
April 21, 19XX

Mr. Craig Schmidt, District Manager
Desert Chicken Shops, Inc.
P.O. Box 6230
Los Angeles, California 98865

Dear Mr. Schmidt:

My four years as a successful restaurant manager and top performer with a nationwide fast-food chain are outlined in the enclosed resume. In 1989 I graduated from Harman University with a degree in restaurant management and a 3.75 GPA.

Your local manager in Espinosa, Rod Sterling, suggested that I forward my resume to you. Desert Chicken's rapid growth and exceptional product quality are well known. It is the kind of organization I would like to grow with. Rod speaks highly of the company's management style.

I will call your office in a few days to schedule a convenient time to meet and discuss some areas of mutual interest.

Thank you very much for your consideration.

Sincerely,

Rick Lampe

Richard Lampe

6345 Highland Boulevard
Minneapolis, Minnesota 55433
March 7, 19XX

Mr. James Blackwell
Vice-President, Engineering
Acme Revolving Door Company
New Brunswick, Pennsylvania

Dear Mr. Blackwell:

I graduated last month from the University of Minnesota with a 3.66 grade point average and a Bachelor of Science degree in mechanical engineering.

Your company was recommended by my uncle, John Blair. He has appreciated your friendship and business relationship over the years and advised me to forward my resume to you.

My objective is to design mechanical parts for a company that enjoys an outstanding reputation for quality and conducts business internationally.

I hope that it will be acceptable for me to call your office to arrange to meet you and discuss possible opportunities with Acme. I plan to be in Pennsylvania toward the end of next month; this might be a convenient time if your schedule permits.

Sincerely,

Patricia McKay

Patricia Anne McKay
(612) 555-3345

Enclosure: resume

642 Miglia Lane
Denver, Colorado
January 5, 19XX

Ms. Barbara Colman
Marketing Manager
Danté Cosmetics
3490 Lasswell Boulevard
Cleveland, Ohio 46782

Dear Ms. Colman:

Margaret Brighton suggested that I contact you and provided me with valuable information about your firm's rapidly growing line of pet cosmetics.

I graduated in December from Cleveland College of Business with an Associate's Degree in accounting and office management. My GPA was 3.87/4.0, and the faculty voted me "Outstanding Student."

My ability with numbers has led me to positions as treasurer for our church and for a regional office management organization, NOMA.

My favorite fields are accounting and cosmetics. Margaret recommended that I contact you to see if you have a few moments to spend with me to review my qualifications and my resume and to see if any possibilities exist for entry-level positions at Danté.

I will call you next week to see if we might meet. Thank you so much for your consideration.

Sincerely,

Roberta G. Mielczarek

Roberta Mielczarek

Enclosure: resume

7235 West Hunter Street
Ocean Shore, Washington 99888
October 14, 19XX

Ms. Eileen Nockman
Oleander Temporary Services
1200 Main Street
Lincoln, Nebraska 67893

Dear Ms. Nockman:

Your advertisement in the Sunday newspaper sounded wonderful! I have heard excellent things about Oleander from Mitch Frommer, my former neighbor. I graduated from Black Hills State University in South Dakota and plan to move to Lincoln next month.

Mitch suggested that I forward my resume when I showed him your ad. (He also volunteered to call you to provide a personal recommendation, which he may have done by now.)

My resume is enclosed. I am interested in being a Service Assistant with Oleander and will call you this week to request an interview. I can drive down any day, any time.

Thanks very much.

Sincerely,

Anne Kawamoto

Anne Kawamoto

Enclosure: resume

3769 Forest View Trail
Trace, Missouri 34512
July 26, 19XX

Mr. Robert Smart
International Sign Company
6535 West Devon Avenue
Chicago, Illinois 60544

Dear Mr. Smart:

Bob Lawrence suggested that I write to see if you might be free for ten minutes or so sometime in the next few weeks. I will be moving to Chicago this weekend and will be living about ten minutes from your office.

Bob, who was my father's college roommate, speaks highly of you and said that I might ask your advice concerning the appearance and content of my resume. In June I graduated from Northwestern University with honors and would appreciate your guidance.

I will call you next week to see when a short meeting might be convenient for you.

Sincerely,

Matt Lenz

Matthew Lenz

Most writers of cover letters make one major mistake above all others. It comes in the closing paragraph.

It is so common that some books written by well-known resume authorities show it as "the correct way." It is not correct.

The mistake is this: In the closing paragraph, the writer mistakenly says:

My home telephone number is 000-0000, and I may be reached there between the hours of 4 and 6 P.M. daily. Please call me to arrange an interview.

In the minds of knowledgeable people, this is a signal that the writer is *lazy*. Why? Because it says:

I'm at home, and I want you to call me if you are interested.

Instead, I recommend that you say you'll call, that you *do* call, and that you *continue* to call, until you get through.

If others are truly eager to call you, they have your number on a resume, or can find it easily enough at the bottom of your letter.

But by your willingness to call, you show a sense of interest, enthusiasm, and a willingness to work that the "you call me" letter writer will never be able to imply.

▶Broadcast Letters

A broadcast letter is a combination cover letter and resume. It is a special letter directed to a specific person, who may be the chief executive officer (CEO), a vice-president, or some other ranking executive of an organization.

It is sometimes called a Marketing Letter because it is used as a part of a "marketing myself" job-hunting campaign.

Some companies specialize in writing a Broadcast Letter for you, typing these in quantity and sending them out to appropriate executives in your chosen field. The fee for composing, printing, and sending these letters can be substantial.

I know of some firms that charge hundreds, even thousands of dollars, for this service. Is it worth the cost? I think not.

Do they work? My opinion is that they do not work well enough to justify the cost for most people. If you wish to consider this technique, read Carl Boll's book, *Executive Jobs Unlimited,* generally considered to be the best book on Broadcast Letters.

Advocates of the Marketing, or Broadcast, Letter claim that it pulls inquiries and responses at double or triple the rate that one can expect when using unsolicited resumes and cover letters.

But resumes and cover letters often pull just one to two percent response, and that means that Broadcast Letters would pull four to six percent at the very best.

The primary advantage of Broadcast/Marketing Letters may lie just in the fact that they are professionally prepared, professionally typed and printed, and *targeted* directly at the leading executives in your field.

Resumes, when sent blindly to personnel offices and recruiters, in quantities large and small, could not be expected to work as well as cleverly targeted Broadcast Letters.

But otherwise, the difference is usually insignificant.

▶ Responding to Want Ads

When you respond to a "help wanted" advertisement, don't expect miracles.

If an ad lists the name of the employer, an address, phone number, and more, you have a reasonable chance at receiving a reply. But don't hold your breath.

Thousands of people will be reading the very same ad, and many employers are overloaded with responses.

Employers run "blind" ads in newspapers and magazines because they want to avoid having to respond to every person who submits a resume. (A *blind ad* is one where the employer is not identified; you will not hear from these employers unless they are interested in you.) Letters, even rejection letters, are expensive to write and send out. Rejection letters might total into the hundreds or thousands from just *one* ad, in *one* paper, on *one* day.

Responses to ads, open or blind, are not always sent immediately, so don't give up hope if you haven't heard from anyone in, say, one or two weeks.

Here's a tip (which we've not seen written anywhere else, but which we have used successfully numerous times):

If you've not heard from the employer, send a second response, exactly the same as the first, with the same resume and the same cover letter. Indicate, with an overprint from your laser printer, or with a tasteful small rubber stamp, that this is a

COPY — ORIGINAL SENT 12/27/94

and affix a neatly written Post-It note, saying, "In case my first resume was lost or didn't arrive, I wanted to be sure you knew of my enthusiasm for this job. Thank you for your consideration." Then sign your name with your first and last names.

Chapter 8
Saying Thank-You &
Following Up

The Impact of Good Manners and Thank-You Notes

Good manners are an important part of the job hunt.

Doing the right thing at the right time will help you get the right job. Failing to do the right thing may well result in your being eliminated along the way, or rejected.

Final selection of the winner from among a group of equally qualified candidates is most often made on "feel," on "fit," and on "how they will get along here."

Well-mannered people whose *actions* communicate their knowledge of what to do and how to handle social situations have a major advantage over others who fail to demonstrate such knowledge.

In this chapter, you learn some of the right techniques to display good manners in the job hunt...and the correct methods for implementing those techniques.

►Thanking People in Your Life

Thanking people is probably the most important factor in the category of good manners. Everyone likes to be thanked.

But usually, job hunters and job applicants are so focused on their *own* problems, strategies, tactics, and activities that they fail to apply good manners as a strategy throughout the job search process.

They are *the* most important factor. Focusing on the other person and treating that person with courtesy, manners, and thoughtfulness will do wonders for increasing the opportunities for success in your job hunt.

Job applicants should *follow through* after an interview. The first step in that *follow through* procedure is to thank the person who interviewed you.

When you're given a gift, you thank the giver. In an interview, you have been given:

- The *time* of the interviewer
- The *hospitality* of the receptionist, the interviewer, and perhaps others
- The *consideration* of the organization to be hired as an employee
- The *information* you received in the interview
- The *opportunity* to possibly be hired and to take an important step in your career

Sequence of a Typical Job-Hunting Situation

The usual sequence of a job-hunting situation:

1. An advertisement appears, or you hear of an opening.
2. You make a phone call to the organization.
3. You submit a resume, cover letter, and possibly examples of your work.
4. You receive an interview appointment (or a rejection).
5. You receive an interview.
6. The employer may follow up with a letter or phone call.
7. If you have been successful, you are probably asked for a second interview.
8. You receive a final offer or polite rejection from the employer.

What's wrong with this "usual" scenario?

You have little or nothing to say about its outcome! This means that results will happen *without* your having anything to say about how things turn out.

That, friends, is where good manners count most. They provide you with that "extra something" so that you will have a major impact on the outcome...and on making that outcome the one *you* want!

How do you do that? It's easy! At the appropriate times, you should respond to an employer's kindness with thank-you notes or cards.

What *are* the appropriate times? They might be situations such as these:

- After the initial phone call to employers, thank them for their kindness and information.
- After the interview, thank them for their time, tour, information, etc.
- After a job offer, thank the initial interviewer and the manager of the department in which you will work.

- After a rejection, thank them for whatever you can…something that was positive and helpful for you in their interview and consideration process.

Sending Thank-You Notes or Cards

There are many good reasons to send thank-you notes:
- You'll feel good when you do.
- The recipient will feel even better than you do.
- It's good manners to do so.
- The recipient will be reminded of you, will think better of you, and will subconsciously be aware of the fact that you "know what to do in social situations."

If an interviewer or manager interviews a few people daily (some interviewers do as many as fifteen interviews on every interview day…some as many as thirty!…and it is definitely, by that time, *not* fun for them to see another applicant), it is important to do whatever you can to be remembered in a positive manner.

Thank-you notes or cards are the easiest, most inexpensive way to do this.

Choosing Notes, Cards, or Stationery—Size, Style, and Color

In stores, you will find cards with "Thank-you" printed, engraved, or embossed thereon.

You'll see other note cards that are plain. Some have borders; others do not. You'll discover that a wide variety of colors is available.

Choose a conservative style, not a loud, wild, or unusual one. Stay away from patterns, illustrations, or trendy designs.

Thank-you notes or plain notes are usually smaller than personal-size stationery and much smaller than business stationery.

Should you use personalized stationery you already own? Probably not. For this special occasion, use something special, something better than ordinary paper for ordinary correspondence. If, however, you happen to have fine-quality paper with superior printing or engraving, and if you know about things like this because of your background, go right ahead and use them. If they are not "the best," however, buy something more distinctive and appropriate.

Choose a plain color, such as white, off-white, cream, ivory, or very light gray. Don't select dark or pastel colors because these are not considered businesslike.

Write your message, a short one, on the bottom part of the inside panel, the one on the bottom after you open the card. If you must, or if your writing is large, you may start at the top and then write on both the top and bottom panels. Do not continue onto the back side.

Do I Write or Print or Type?

Thank-you notes, cards, and other personal styles of correspondence should be personally written. If your handwriting is good, use it.

How do you know if your writing is good enough? If people occasionally compliment you on your handwriting, it is probably good enough; if they do not, be cautious about writing by hand.

If your handwriting isn't good, you have a decision to make. The next best thing for you to do is to *print* your thank-you by hand. If both your cursive handwriting and your printed characters are terrible, you should type it.

But don't type on the notes we've been discussing. Save your typing for business-size stationery (8½" x 11").

▶Some Tips on Writing Good Thank-You Notes

Here are some tips that should help you be #1!

DO. Address the note "Dear Mr. or Ms." rather than use his or her first name. This is proper even if the interviewer has invited you to call him or her by a first name. Obviously, if the interviewer is a personal friend or acquaintance of you and your family, and if you have known the person for years, you may use whatever name you normally call the person, if you feel comfortable in doing so for this business situation.

DO. Keep your note short. This is *not* the time to rehash everything you discussed in an interview, nor is it the time to bring up something you had previously neglected to mention.

DO. Write about something special, if you can. Bring up something that relates specifically to *you* and *your* interview, and which may not relate to all the other applicants.

DO. Spell everything correctly. One misspelled word can torpedo your chances. If you're not a good speller (many otherwise-bright people are not!), check each word of your spelling with a dictionary or with a friend who is a "born speller."

DO. Time your thank-you note to arrive on a good day. How can you know this? If the interviewer tells you that he or she will be talking to candidates over the next three weeks, wait a few days before mailing your note. If the person plans to make a decision in 48 hours, you should write the note immediately and take it to a postal facility where the note will be processed within a few hours. Or drop it off yourself.

DO. Put your return address on the envelope. On a small envelope, it belongs on the back; on a business envelope, it can be written on the back or in the upper-left corner of the front side.

DO. Put adequate postage on the envelope. If you don't, it may result in your envelope being returned to you (a possibly fatal delay!) or delivered "postage due," which the employer will not smile about.

DO. Use an attractive commemorative postage stamp. Studies prove that attractive stamps used in direct-mail advertising result in greater sales. Do *not* use a postage meter for personal correspondence. This not only is improper, but also may lead the recipient to conclude that you are using "company postage for your personal use."

DON'T. Use politically controversial stamps for postage, decoration, or sealing the flap on the reverse side. The person opening your letter may not be as interested in "Free South Africans" as you are.

DO. Use a good-quality pen with a business-color ink—preferably dark blue or black.

DON'T. Oversell yourself! The purpose of this note, card, or letter is to thank, not to sell. Avoid cliches, such as:

I'm the best person to do this job!

Hire me, and you'll never be sorry.
I'm inexperienced, but I'm eager!
I'll work for nothing if you only give me a chance!
Please give me this job. I need it!

DO. Sign your formal name or your conversational name—the name you were called in the interview—when writing a note by hand.

DO. Type your formal name; then sign your conversational name if you are typing a letter.

▶Some Sample Thank-You Notes

Here are a few sample notes and letters for you to use for ideas when you compose your own.

After an interview:

April 22, 19XX

Dear Mr. Nelson,

Thanks so much for seeing me while I was in town last week. I appreciate your kindness, the interview, and all the information you gave me.

I will call you again in a few weeks to see if any openings have developed in your marketing research department's planned expansion.

Appreciatively,

Phil Simmons

Phil Simmons

After an interview:

September 17, 19XX

Mr. Bill Kenner
Sales Manager
WRTV
Rochester, Minnesota

Dear Mr. Kenner:

Thank you very much for the interview and the market information you gave me yesterday. I was most impressed with the city, your station, and everyone I met.

As you requested, I am enclosing a resume and have asked my ex-manager to call you on Tuesday, the 21st, at 10:00 a.m.

Working at WRTV with you and your team would be both interesting and exciting for me. I look forward to your reply and to the possibility of helping you set new records for next year.

Sincerely,

Anne Bently

Anne Bently
1434 River Drive
Polo, Washington 99654

Informal note to a network member:

October 14, 19XX

Dear Bill,

I really appreciate your recommending me to Alan Stevens at Wexler Cadillac.

We met yesterday for almost an hour, and we're having lunch again Friday.

If this develops into a job offer, as I think it may, I will be most grateful.

Enclosed is a copy of a reference letter by my summer employer. I thought you might find it helpful.

You're a good friend, and I appreciate your thinking of me.

Sincerely,

Dave

Dave

After an interview:

July 26, 19XX

Dear Ms. Bailey,

Thank you for the interview for the auditor's job last week.

I appreciate the information you gave me and the opportunity to interview with John Peters. He asked me for a transcript, which I am forwarding today.

Working in my field of finance in a respected firm such a Barry Productions appeals to me greatly.

I appreciate your consideration and look forward to hearing from you.

Sincerely,

Dan Rehling

Dan Rehling

After an interview and before another interview:

May 21, 19XX

Ms. Sandra Waller
Yellow Side Stores
778 Northwest Boulevard
Seattle, Washington 99659

Dear Ms. Waller:

Thank you so much for the interview you gave me last Friday for the Retail Management Training Program. I learned a great deal and know now that retailing is my first choice for a career.

I am looking forward to interviewing with Mr. Daniel and Ms. Sobczak next week.

For that meeting, I will bring two copies of my resume and a transcript, as you suggested.

Enclosed is a copy of a reference letter written by my summer employer. I thought you might find the letter helpful.

Sincerely,

Elizabeth Duncan

Elizabeth Duncan

After a phone call and before the interview:

March 22, 19XX

Dear Ms. Samson,

Thanks for talking with me by phone today. You made me feel at ease!

I appreciate your granting me an interview appointment and look forward to meeting you in your office at 10:00 a.m. on Tuesday, March 29.

I will bring my design portfolio with me. Thanks again.

Sincerely,

Bradley Kurtz

Bradley Kurtz

►Follow Up!

Have you ever been disappointed with the actions—or inactions—of other people, or with their dependability or undependability?

Of course! That is the way most people lead their lives, and that is exactly the way most people conduct their job hunt.

They fail to take responsibility to follow up, follow through, and do what they say they will do.

Imagine what possibilities arise when you do things that other people fail to do…which other candidates-for-employment fail to do…and which employers themselves would never imagine that candidates would do!

Follow up. Follow through. Do what others do not do. Do what others do not think about doing.

Following Up before an Interview

After you make a phone call to an employer, when that employer has invited you to an interview, you might use one of these methods to follow through:

- Write a confirming letter or note of thanks, restating the time when you will be there.
- Call the person's assistant or secretary, probably one or two days before the date of the interview, inquiring whether the time is still convenient and asking any other questions you may have (for example, travel directions).

Do not call the person with whom you will be interviewing. This would be considered "overkill" and might create a negative "who does this person think he (or she) is?" impression.

Following Up after an Interview

Send a thank-you note, of course. Be certain it creates a good impression and that it is appropriate, both to you and to the situation.

Do not include any other information with the thank-you note. That would be considered "mixing business activities with personal activities."

Other material (transcripts, reference letters, photocopies of credentials, etc.) should be sent separately in a larger envelope. These things should always be accompanied by some type of correspondence, even if it is only a Post-It Note or a short letter of transmittal.

Following Up after Being Rejected

Should you follow up after being rejected? Logic, common sense, and your own personal pride all tell you, *"no!"*

This isn't necessarily true. In fact, if you are being creative in your job hunt, you will think "possibility," not "no possibility." Failing to contact the employer is "no possibility" thinking.

Those who *do* follow up often do so for the wrong reason: to find out why they were rejected. To find out what they did *wrong*.

Will most employers tell them where they went wrong? No. And rarely will they tell the *whole* truth. After all, it isn't always in an employer's best interest to tell someone that he or she had bad breath or body odor, wore dirty clothes, had dirty hair, wasn't appropriately dressed, had bad taste, or displayed poor manners.

So when you do follow up after being rejected, do this:

- Thank the employer for the interviewing process (again); for the consideration you received (again); for any additional materials, interviews, meals, or hospitality you have received since your first written thank-you…and that's all.
- Then, to open the domain of "possibility" for yourself, restate your interest in other opportunities in the organization for yourself. Restate this in "one" sentence, in a very enthusiastic manner, but don't do it *at length.* Keep it short!
- Finally, close with a "possibility" statement, such as "I would like the opportunity to stay in touch with you over the next few months. Thanks very much for everything."

This allows you the option you want. Instead of the door being closed, it is now open.

"What good will this do me?"

Perhaps none. But perhaps much. I know cases where a reopened door led to an immediate reconsideration of the candidate: "If he really liked us that much, maybe we should hire him."

Or it left the door open so that when the organization's first-choice candidate rejected the offer she received, the possibility had already been created to call their second choice: the person who's "so interested in us that she sent a letter restating how enthusiastic she is about us."

Following Up with Your Network

Every few weeks, it's a good idea to follow up, in writing or by phone, with important people in your network.

Following up means staying in touch with them, not to see if they can do anything for you. And not to see if they have done anything for you.

It means staying in touch to see how they are, to inquire about how their family is, or how their organization's sales or services are coming along, and perhaps to thank them for anything they might have done for you or for any advice they may have given along the way.

If what they have done is to provide support for you, to be "thinking positively for you toward the possibility of getting the job and the opportunity you want," then the purpose for your call or note is to acknowledge them for that support.

Your contact with them might take other forms. Try one or more of these in your stay-in-touch-with-your network plan:

- Send a magazine article that interests you and which would definitely interest them.
- Send an article that interests them, but which holds no interest for you.
- Send a cartoon or a few cartoons or jokes (in good taste, please!) that are likely to produce a smile or a laugh from them.
- Call with some new information that you have uncovered about a topic which interests him or her, or which interests both of you.

By staying in touch, perhaps every few weeks, and by being *focused on the other person* rather than on your own needs and wants, you will achieve what you want.

What you want...is for the recipient to think, if only for few seconds, or moments, about you...to think about what a nice person you are...and about the possibility that they might be able to help or respond to you in some way.

Following Up and Staying in Control

During your job hunt, *you* should remain in control.

Most job hunters think they have no control. They think "circumstances" have control...that "employers" are in control...that "the organizations" have the power and the control.

But organizations exist only because people are in them and because people often need to be served by them. And you, friend, are those "people." So you *have* the control.

In the job hunt, you must not give up all control.

One of the major mistakes is to expect employers to call you instead of realizing that you must call them. Most cover letters conclude with "My number is 000-0000, and I may be reached between X a.m. and X p.m."

The moment you ask them to call you, instead of your calling them, you've lost control.

Waiting for the telephone to ring is not part of your job hunt campaign. It puts you *out* of control. It prevents you from being *pro*active and requires you to be *re*active.

In your letter, say that *you* will call. In the interview, thank them for offering to call, but ask if you might call them instead.

When you call, you may not get through. Call again. Continue to call until you get through. Leave your name, but never leave your number.

When you leave your number, you've lost control.

After several unsuccessful attempts to talk to the person you want to reach, you might consider asking, "When is a good time to reach her for a one-minute phone conversation? I've tried different times and haven't had much luck?"

Following Up by Creating the Environment

When you call back, as opposed to someone else calling you, you have an opportunity to "create the environment" for your call.

If the other person calls you, your kids may be screaming. Or you may be testing the *loudness* control on your stereo. Or your dog may be barking. Even worse, you may be arguing with someone and in a mood you would prefer to hide from others.

When you call them, create a *quiet* environment. Focus on them, on what you will say, on being alert and pleasant, and on eliminating possibilities for a negative environment:

- Send the kids outside.
- Turn off the radio and the stereo.
- Turn off the TV!
- Have paper and pen handy.
- Be in sight of the door, so that you can see and be warned about approaching visitors.
- Don't be eating, drinking, or chewing gum.
- Have a glass of water handy, in case you need it.

- Be clear about the purposes of your call—use notes written down about what you will say, what questions you want answered.
- Ask if the person you reach "has a minute or two to talk right now?"
- Always give your name slowly, clearly, distinctly. Remind the other person of who you are and what you are there for, and do it all slowly!
- Smile! Keep both your physical and your mental selves *happy!*
- When you conclude, stay in control. If someone tells you, "We'll call you if we get anything," ask if you might call that person again sometime, "because I'm gone quite a bit." Then call again or write again, to stay in touch and to find out about that person, not about what is coming up for you.

▶Keep Smiling

In the course of following up and following through, you'll be rejected. You won't get through. You won't be acknowledged for the wonderful person you are.

Whatever happens, keep smiling!

Whatever your problems may be, don't talk about them. Remember: other people are not particularly interested in your problems. They're interested in their own.

So focus on other people. And sound happy, enthusiastic, and pleasant. Not eager, not pushy, not needing or wanting...just happy and competent.

So S-M-I-L-E, and you'll come across the way you want to come across.

Chapter 9
Job Search Tips

Additional Tips for Your Job Search

In this book, I've provided a variety of ways to help you create a resume that will be attractive to the eye, easy to read, easy to skim, elegant to touch, and which contains the kind of substance employers are looking for when selecting new employees.

But your resume is for your job search. So here is a review of the job search advice given throughout this book, as well as a few new tips.

Private Employment Services

Private employment agencies fill a small percentage of jobs filled annually throughout North America.

Some experts say the number is as low as 2 percent or 5 percent.

One five-person agency in a medium-sized American city of 600,000 people placed a total of 26 people in 1987. From this small amount of activity/results, all five people made a living and supported their families.

The numbers required to "be successful" as a placement person in a private employment agency are *much* smaller than you might expect.

What are your odds, then? Small. Very small. Slight. Very slight.

Should you, then, give up on agencies?

No. But give them what they deserve: a small amount of your time…and do *not* depend on them.

▶ State Employment Services

The 50 employment services, one in each state, and the similar organizations in Canada, in each province, are also known as "the unemployment offices" in most states and provinces.

The name might be appropriate. Unemployment compensation checks and applications are handled in another department, but the term "unemployment" fits more often than "employment."

Should you give up on state or provincial employment offices?

Probably. They may be worth a small amount of your time. But not much.

One study quoted in *What Color Is Your Parachute?* shows that most people placed (relatively few *are* placed from the large pool of applicants received by these government offices) were not working at their new jobs after just thirty days!

So the offices, while they *did* place some of their applicants, were, in effect, acting as "temporary help agencies," i.e., placing people on jobs where they remained for only a short time.

Don't depend on them.

▶ Personnel Offices

When I was Corporate Director of Personnel, in charge of all recruiting, screening, and hiring, I thought that those three activities constituted "what I did for a living" and "what I do at work."

Wrong.

What I did at work was to:

- Recruit large numbers of people for jobs.
- Eliminate large numbers of people from consideration for jobs.
- Send final candidates to department heads for further screening out and semi-rejection from our view—permanent and final rejection from each candidate's view.
- Ultimately reject all but one candidate for each job.

What I *really* did, then, was to spend *most* of my time *rejecting* candidates.

So although my title was OK and acceptable, what I actually *did*, from most people's point of view, is now deemed UNacceptable.

That is, when I admit to people, now, that my primary duty, that the activity in which I spent a most of my time…was that of *rejection,* those people utter some quite nasty remarks:

- "Don't you think that was unfair?"
- "Didn't you miss some awfully good candidates for employment if you stopped reading resumes after you had 'enough good ones to pick from'?"
- "If you were looking for *reasons to reject candidates,* wasn't your attitude quite negative?"
- "Why didn't you look for the good things rather than the bad things?"

We do, of course, look for the good things.

All interviewers, screeners, recruiters, and personnel people look for the best traits we can find in people.

We first screen in the qualified people—those who have the right educational background and required technical knowledge for the department in which they might work.

But once we get enough of those candidates, we must look for things that will eliminate *some* of them from the running.

And when one is looking for reasons to eliminate people, those reasons are usually negative ones.

*ASIDE: By not even considering some people with less-than-the-minimum experience or educational background, aren't we, **again,** missing the possibility of some excellent candidates?*

Yes. Of course, we are! But we can't see *everyone.*

We can see only a few. So, unfair as it is, we draw lines. Some people get in. Others are left out.

Understand that personnel offices deal with *many* people. Sometimes, they lose their cool. Sometimes, they don't treat you fairly. Sometimes, they seem to act as though they don't even care if you get a job there or not. Sometimes, they aren't polite. Sometimes, they forget who you are. Sometimes, they goof up and fail to write you, or call you, or invite you.

Bounce back.

Understand those things, and then go on with dealing with the office.

Or, if you want my best advice, avoiding dealing with them completely.

After all, they are in the *rejection business,* not the *hiring business.*

The person in the *hiring business* is the one who gets to see the *few* candidates after the Personnel Department *rejects* the *many* candidates.

So if you can eliminate the step called The Personnel Department, or the Personnel Interview, or The Screening Interview, or The Initial Interview, do so!

ASIDE: In recent years, the numbers of large companies have been decreasing, and the numbers of small companies have been increasing.

Studies show that most job opportunities, most *new* jobs created in our fast-moving, fast-changing economy, come from organizations that have 100 employees or fewer, and that most of those jobs come from organizations that have fewer than 20 employees.

And more than 2/3 of our workers, nationwide, in the USA, now work in small businesses—that is, in companies that have fewer than 250 employees.

When you next read about plans being made for large companies, notice this: those plans almost always include "downsizing" instead of "increasing the number of employees."

Do these smaller companies *have* Personnel Departments?

No.

Most do not. This is especially true of the 20-or-fewer category, but it is true of the 100-or-fewer and even of the 250-or-fewer, too.

In these firms, managers, executives, and line-management people do the selecting and hiring, rather than staff people, in a Personnel or Human Resources Department.

Use your networking abilities to get to know someone in the field, in the company, in the city, in a church, who can get you to the person who is in *charge of hiring*...and forget about trying to see the person who is *in charge of rejection.*

And do not stop until you get to know who they are, until you get to meet or talk with them, and until you get the opportunity to present yourself, *very carefully,* in person.

That, my friends, is the way people get hired...and the way people avoid being summarily rejected.

►Applications

If you do go through The Personnel Department, do so carefully.

Be nice, even if members of the department are not.

Be well-dressed, neat, and clean, even if they are not.

Be on time, even if they are not.

Be well-prepared and know about their organization, even if they appear to know nothing about you...and appear to care even less.

Do whatever you must to be certain you are *the #1 candidate* when you present yourself at, in, or through The Personnel Department.

Remember, the persons there are not seeing only "you." They are, at the same moment, comparing you to "all the others."

And before you get angry about this, remember that YOU do it, too, or...at least, you DID, when you were dating, or choosing friends, or choosing a church, or selecting a TV.

We all do it.

So just *understand* that "WE ALL DO IT," and be the best-prepared candidate you can be.

Be Prepared

When you go to The Personnel Department, prepare beforehand.

- Read about the organization. Don't complain that you can't; just do it.

- Scout the route. Know how you'll get there and how long it will take. A half hour early is fine, but one minute late is *deadly.*

- Be nice to the greeter/receptionist. That person has more power in his or her little finger, or writing hand, or in one or two words spoken to the interviewer, than you have, even if you made $250,000 last year!

- Be well dressed. Not adequately dressed, but well dressed. The #1 candidate is never hired because he or she is "adequate."

- Be at ease. If you know the organization, or have read about it, you'll be closer to being at ease than if you have no knowledge.

- Go to the bathroom before you arrive. If drinking coffee is likely to require your presence in a bathroom, do not drink coffee.

- If you are carrying materials, a portfolio, papers, or credentials with you to the interview, they should be carried in something classy, not something chintzy. If you are using an attache case, it should be relatively slender and not chock-full of stuff. (Thick attache cases are for students who carry their books to class or for door-to-door salespeople.)

- Do not carry cigarettes with you. And do not smoke, either outside or inside the interview room, even if you are offered the opportunity to do so. Of those who smoke, few do it well.

- Do not chew gum. Anywhere. Ever.

- Be clean. Fingers, hands, face, hair, body.

- Have your clothes clean. Unwrinkled. Shoes shined.

- Be well-groomed. If you're a male, consider shaving your beard and mustache. If you're a female, look like a female from *Working Woman* magazine rather than from *Glamour* or *Vogue*.

- Don't be nervous. Ask your friends if you have nervous or annoying mannerisms, and invite them to be brutal in telling you about it.

- Better to be aware of the problem and to handle it . . than to be rejected in your ignorance of the matter.

Filling Out Applications

Everyone hates filling out applications.

And once you've filled out a dozen or so, you hate it even more.

Some of them are one page long, and some are eight pages long.

They are *all* "no fun."

But they "are required."

They are part and parcel of The Personnel Department.

So when you go, go early enough if you know you will be required to fill out the application.

If your handwriting is bad, *print.* If your printing is bad, print *slowly* and *neatly.* You *can* do it! If you go slowly enough, you *can* make your characters *neat* and *attractive.* So just *do it!*

Because doing it neatly is *required.*

If you need background information about yourself that you have not memorized—or about your previous employers, including company names and addresses and the names of your supervisors—bring that information with you. Put it on sheets of paper and place them in your classy carrier, attache case, or briefcase.

If you dislike the questions on the application, you have several choices.

First, you can get angry and not answer them.

But answering them is *required.* So the result of that action will be *rejection.* Rejection-with-anger, by the way, is less productive than *nice rejection.*

Nice Rejection can mean "Possibility." Rejection-with-anger always means "No possibility."

Second, you can become angry, conquer your anger, become OK with your thoughts, and then answer the questions that angered you. So the organization will get the answers they need, and you will no longer be angry.

Third, you can decide that you don't want to work for a company that asks those kinds of questions.

In that case, you leave.

This is also called "No possibility."

But it might be a pretty good idea.

Bad Questions on applications can come from intent or ignorance.

If they come from ignorance, it's no big deal. We're all ignorant once in a while.

But if the Bad Questions come from intent, then perhaps you are in the wrong place for an application-and-interview.

So if you decide to leave, you are opening the space for someone who isn't quite so bright, or discerning, or choosy, or fussy as you are. So be it.

The Last Word on Filling Out Applications

Applications are used for screening people out, just as resumes are.

So fill out applications carefully in a manner that will allow you to be *in* rather than *out of* consideration.

If the application says "Salary Expected" or "Salary Desired," write the word *"open."* Don't put an amount.

A specific amount can get you *in consideration* very quickly, but for a smaller amount of money than employers might otherwise have been willing to pay you...before they discovered the paltry amount you would be willing to work for!

Disclose nothing that you know can eliminate you from being *in consideration.*

Do not be cryptic. Do not say "Personal" in reply to questions.

In short, use common sense. Most job applicants do not. They use Fog Logic, not Clear Logic.

Be clear and view your application from the employer's point of view—the reader's point of view.

Tell things that will keep you *in consideration* and prevent you from being eliminated.

Common sense? Absolutely.

Commonly done? No.

Be creative. Be clever. Be hired.

▶ The Road Less Traveled: A More Effective Way

Find out what everyone else is doing.

Then do something else.

Something different. Something better. Something creative.

Are there better ways than "the way everyone tells me to do my job hunt"?

As you read in the first chapter, and as some of you have heard, there may be. My feeling is that there *is.*

What you do in your job hunt is a function, of course, of what you already know.

In this book, you learned a very different way to look at resumes. You saw a way that focuses not on you, but on the person doing the skimming, the reading, and the selecting.

If job applicants are going through the motions of writing a resume so that they can send out five hundred, get twelve replies, have six interviews, receive two offers, and then choose between them, those people shouldn't bother with this book.

Neither should they bother with this chapter.

But if you understand *now* that what you *do* in your life and job hunt is a function of what you *know,* you might be interested in *knowing* a bit more.

Here it is. A set of creative ideas to help your job hunt result in success…and in your achieving *aliveness* in the job you land…a job you truly love. A job you look forward to. A job you're so eager for, that you'd gladly go there and do it for nothing!

▶ Networking—When It Works and When It Doesn't

Networking, used correctly, can help you achieve exactly what you want.

But only if you *know* exactly what you want.

So before you follow Yuppie advice and "network yourself like crazy," understand two things:

- Getting help from others in your network requires you to give help to others in your network…and to others not currently in your network. Successful living is a give-and-take situation, and it works better if you give *more* than you take, or expect to take.

- Individuals in your network *want* to help you. But only if you make it relatively easy. And only if you've done your part of the work "first."

Asking *me* to get *you* a job isn't the idea. Not at all.

But giving me the opportunity to help you, help me, and help a friend of mine: that's the idea of a network and networking, applied properly.

Before you network, know what you want to *do*. Know what skills you have. Know what problems those skills can solve. Know the areas in which you would like to apply those skills to solve specific problems.

Know *all* those things.

Then, only then, start to call on your network.

First: Friends and Relatives

Call on friends and relatives first. Call especially on people for whom you have done favors.

Let them know your objectives, skills, talents, abilities, and interests.

Then ask them if they know anyone who is *already doing* what you want to do…using the skills you plan to use.

It would be nice if that person is applying his or her skills in a field that interests you strongly. But even if that's not the case, even if that person is applying the skills in a field that doesn't interest you at all, take the next step.

The next step is to see if your friend or relative would, on your behalf, arrange a meeting among the three of you—a lunch, an after-work snack or sandwich, a chat at your friend's home, or anything that brings you together socially.

The purpose of the meeting is for you to learn what your contact person is doing and how he or she likes it. Does that person like the place he or she is working, and does he or she know anyone or any organization who is working in the field you're aiming for…and who may have need for a person with your skills…or who may have the kinds of problems you're capable of solving?

Then follow up, follow through. Network again to meet the people your contact person knows, and continue to do this.

At each step along the way, *thank* people. Use your good manners. Send notes, even to your relative or friend whom you see regularly.

Thank the third person, the friend-of-your-relative, too. Write a note. Stay in touch. Keep thanking people. Keep validating them…helping them know that they count…that they've done a good turn.

You'll find that networking works wonders. It can get you into places and into organizations you'd never know about or imagine that you could penetrate.

Most of you got most of *your* jobs through friends, relatives, and acquaintances.

So use the strategy to get your next job, too.

Twenty-eight percent of all people, at the minimum, get their jobs through friends, relatives, and acquaintances.

That's more than twice the number of those who admit to getting their jobs through a newspaper classified ad.

So if it works twice as well, give it twice the effort.

Develop New "Acquaintances"

It's not only "who you know."

It's who you will take the trouble to meet from now on.

So create a new network. A better network.

If, at the places where you've been going, the people you've been hanging out with haven't been supporting your goals and objectives to get where you want to go in your life and your career, it might be time to add a new friend or two to the group.

One way to do this easily is to get new names, and names of new social organizations, from people you already know. Branch out, just as a tree does. Grow a new branch from one that already exists.

And if you need or want to make a clean break, join new groups. Attend a different church of your denomination. Go to groups as a guest of your friends. Network there, too.

How?

Listen to people. Ask questions of people. Don't pester them to death with talk about yourself.

Listeners go over much bigger than talkers do.

That's especially true for the first few times you meet someone.

Be interested in them, instead of concentrating on impressing them with how interesting you are…what you've done…where you've been…how wonderful you are…and especially with "the bad breaks you've had."

Ask questions. Then listen. Agree. Acknowledge. Be interested. (Who knows? You might even learn something!)

The more branches you add to your tree, the better and stronger your network will be.

Get Referrals to Supervisors and Managers, Too

In addition to talking to people who are doing what you want to do, who are using the skills you want to use on a job, don't omit supervisors and managers.

Network your way to them, too.

Why? Because supervisors and managers are the ones who must plan for the future of their organizations...the ones who have the headaches of "personnel problems," the problems of people who aren't doing their jobs...who quit...who became ill and are unable to do their jobs...and who, then, have *big problems.*

If you come along, and if you get to know those supervisors, you may turn out to be the solution to one of those problems.

If that is true, you'll be pleasantly surprised at how easy it is to get hired. In fact, you might find it difficult to "get away."

▶Ask for an Interview Even If There Are No Openings

Interviewing when there are no jobs is *not* a waste of time.

No jobs today? Maybe jobs tomorrow.

Ask for an interview. Afterward, thank the person in writing. Ask questions in the interview. Show you are interested. Read up on the company and the field before you go in, so that you can ask intelligent questions, not stupid questions about health insurance, vacations, and fringe benefits.

Stay in touch afterward. Let prospective employers know you're interested.

How about the "sneak-in" interview, the one advocated by people who say you should try to get in for an interview by asking for "advice" or by asking someone to "evaluate my resume" when you are *really* looking for "a job"!

Sorry, folks. Honesty really does pay.

Don't lie to get in to see someone. They're smarter than you think, and you are likely to get "permanently UNhired" by that organization when the person discovers you've "sneaked in."

This isn't networking.

Networking is something that works for everyone, not just for you.

▶Keep Following Up

Stay in touch with people in your network.

Send thank-you notes.

Send cartoons. Or articles from professional journals.

Don't be a pest. Don't be "too aggressive." Once in a while is enough. That means once every month or so.

Find ways to stay in touch. Be creative.

Send Resumes

Just because you've sent one resume doesn't mean the employer still has it.

Just because it has been sent it to someone else, doesn't mean that the other person has it.

It probably has been lost.

Remind the first reader. Send another resume.

Attach a note:

Thanks again for considering my resume. In case you need another, here's an extra copy.

Call!

Call again. Call to see if the reader needs more information. Call to see if there's anything else you should be doing. Call to see if you need to contact references. Or to get transcripts or credentials.

Call to see when you should call the next time.

If you detect a tone of annoyance in the voice of a secretary, manager, or supervisor, say that you don't want to call too frequently, but that you are usually away from a phone and wanted to be certain you made yourself available. You may show, through an occasional phone call, just how interested you really are in the opportunity with that organization.

Send Notes

Remember, send *good* notes. Short notes. Classy notes. And flawless notes, without smudges or dirt.

Notes and stationery should be "in good taste." If you somehow skipped over Chapter 5 ("Packaging and Delivering a Resume"), go back and read it.

And always—in writing, in person, or in social gatherings—be *seen and heard* "in good taste."

One 44-year-old university business administration graduate, retired from the armed services, and recently retrained in his newly chosen field of computer science, decided to be seen everywhere...to "network his way to a job" after other methods had failed him.

This is usually a good idea.

But he executed it poorly.

He wore a cheap polyester suit and a wide polyester tie, years after wide ties were passe. (Polyester ties are "always" passe!)

He wore long sideburns, which is fine for a costume party, bad for business.

Two years later, after hundreds of applications and interviews, and after networking his way through every organization in his city, he's still without a job in his field of computer science.

He looks like a "2" when he could look like a "10." He talks when he should listen. And he brags about his service experiences, instead of asking "I'm interested in you" questions of the people he meets.

He's a loser. But even worse: he doesn't know it.

▶ Use the *Yellow Pages*

If you run out of ideas, use the *Yellow Pages* as a source of ideas.

You'll see how many thousands of places there are, how many thousands of jobs exist, and you'll get ideas about networking, people to contact, and even places to visit.

Should you write to places you see listed in the *Yellow Pages?*

Not if you can *network* your way to meet people who work there.

Always go through someone you know, to get to see or meet or visit with someone, or some place, you do not know.

Don't "go in cold," without an introduction, unless you've failed miserably to network your way into a contact.

Going in cold usually results in failure, especially if you're looking for favors, time, or interviews, or if you should wander in at a particularly busy time.

►Walk In, Anyway

Want to try it now? Just going in cold?

Try this, if you must:

- Prepare. Read about the company, the field. Or go in, ask for information about the organization, and then leave until you've had a chance to read the information at home.

- Look good. Dress up, not down. Remember that dressing up is a way of paying respect to the people you're visiting, or people you are with.

- Tell the receptionist, truthfully, that this kind of firm interests you, that you have been reading about it, and that you're considering entering a company like this as a career, as the next step.

- Ask if there is anyone in the firm you might talk to. See if anyone might have 10 minutes to spare for you so that you could learn a bit more than you've read about.

- If the receptionist is friendly and helpful, thank him or her for the assistance. Get the receptionist's name; then thank the person in writing as soon as you get home.

- The same goes for the person you talk to about the company. Thank her or him, in writing, as soon as you return home.

- In your 10-minute chat, ask questions about what you've learned in your reading.

- Ask how the company hires new employees. Ask if interviews are held regularly. Ask how you might obtain an interview to be considered for any new positions that might be opening up.

- Ask how you might learn more. Are there publications you might read? Is there a company newsletter, national, regional, or local? Might you have a copy of his or her business card?

- Thank! In person...and in writing.

►Some Tips for Negotiating Salary

Information about salary is sometimes difficult to come by.

If you go into an interview with *no* salary information, you deal from a position of weakness.

You should go into any interview with salary information about at least three things:

- Salary information about the field you're interested in

- Salary information about the particular organization you're interviewing with

- Salary information about other organizations in the same business as the organization you're interviewing with

ASIDE: *People, and out-of-work job applicants in particular, usually assume that they are out of control in the matter of salaries. This is not necessarily true.*

If people are employed, and paid, to solve problems, the question becomes "What is it worth to the employer to solve this problem?" rather than "What will they pay me?"

No matter what skills you will be using on this job or any job...someone else, in some other organization or in some other situation, will use those identical skills to solve the same or a very similar problem, and that person will be paid very, very well!

Your "Thinking" puts you "In Control" or "Out of Control" in the matter of salaries (and everything else!).

If you are thinking only within a small universe of Thinking and Possibility, the salary you will be able to command will be small, and there will be no possibility for it to be large.

To increase your "Possibility of a large salary and huge earnings," you must enlarge your Thinking.

You must continue to increase your skills, your knowledge, and your worth.

When you begin to think that "I know enough now and don't need to know any more," you have put a cap on your Thinking...and on your potential earnings.

This small section, these words above, are well worth the price of this entire book. They are, in fact, priceless.

But only if you use them.

Salaries and Earnings in Your Chosen Field

How do people in your field earn their living?

Are they salaried? Are they paid on the basis of their output, their production? Do they receive bonuses? For what? Are their salaries reviewed? How often?

There are *many* more questions to ask than these.

Create some of your own.

Write down the things you would like to know about salaries, earnings, bonuses, and potential earnings in your chosen field.

You should go into any interview with knowledge of the going rate for the industry and for specific jobs within that industry, plus knowledge of the growth factors and the nongrowth factors.

You can obtain this information from the library. Or from your state or provincial employment service.

Know the ranges, from entry-level positions to positions at the very top.

If you go into an interview without this information, you will be Out of Control.

Psychologists would say you are "at effect" rather than "at cause."

Know what salary information you want. Then find it.

How Does This Organization Pay Its People?

Companies and organizations do not willingly give out salary information.

In fact, some organizations have been known to fire employees who violate a signed agreement that states:

"I will not discuss my earnings with my fellow workers inside this organization or with people outside this organization."

How, then do you find out? From friends, relatives, neighbors, or colleagues.

Don't crassly ask, "How much money do people like you make?"

But do ask light, tactful questions such as "How much do you think someone in this position might make at ABC Distributors? Is there any way to find out what they pay, and what the earnings potential is at ABC?"

Any organization's pay scale is part of its reputation.

If you ask around, ask enough people, and if you ask tactfully, you *can* find out the answers.

If you go into an interview without knowing, you haven't done enough homework or research, and you will not be In *Full* Control.

Salary Information in Other Organizations

The more you know about what other organizations are paying their people, the more control you will have in the interview with your chosen organization…or, at least, in the interview with whatever company you're lucky enough to have an interview with.

This, too, you can discover through the public or university libraries in your city, through books written about salaries in various fields, or from the local office of your state or provincial job/employment/unemployment office.

▶How to Answer "The Big Question"

After a pleasant, possibly successful interview, The Big Question usually comes up.

You *hope* it comes up.

If it does, you can usually conclude that "they're interested in me."

The Big Question, of course, is this:

"How much money are you looking for?"

If they ask you this, they're usually interested.

It's possible they're not interested and are merely collecting information so that they will be able to offer their #1 candidate an appropriate salary, but *usually,* it means "We're interested."

How do you answer the tough question, "How much will you take?"

If you've not done your homework or research, if you do not know salary information about the job, the company and the field, the likelihood is that you will not do very well in your reply.

Do the research, so that you can be In Control.

If you know the information, you can answer the question this way: you can provide information, not merely a reply.

Employers always like information. They appreciate it, and if you can enlighten them about an important subject, you, too, will be appreciated.

You do *not* want to answer the question directly. You do not want, then, to "name an amount of money."

Everything "depends." In life, everything "depends."

Life is full of trade-offs.

So, too, is your job and the job offer you are negotiating for.

It might be the best job in the world, but for $8,000 annually, it wouldn't be.

It might be fun, but if you're working with dolts, with narrow-minded people, it wouldn't be.

So provide information...information that will allow the other person in the room to "handle the situation about your salary situation."

Here are *good* ways to answer the "How much money are you looking for?" question:

- "The job is much more important to me than the money is."

- "This organization is exactly what I am looking for."

- "I've been doing some salary research, a personal project, on my own...just to be aware of what's going on in the field and to see what people with my kind of background are worth these days."

- "From what I've been able to find out, by researching and by talking to people in the field, it seems that *most* of the people with my kind of background and experience and talents and skills...that **most** of those people...are starting out, the people at my level, somewhere in the neighborhood of _____ to _____."

ASIDE: The two numbers you should mention are those that constitute a range of salaries. Be truthful: mention the almost-lowest amount and the highest amount you've discovered that people are earning in this job, solving these kinds of problems.

You can include, or not include, fringe benefits and bonuses in these amounts. Use your discretion in making the decision to include or not include these factors.

The interviewer's question to you was: "How much do you want?"

Have you answered it?

No.

But you have provided some *information,* some excellent *guidelines,* for him or her to conclude that (1) you are interested; (2) you are somewhat flexible and not rigid; (3) the negotiations can now begin; and (4) you have provided, by stating information, a framework for the negotiations...and made the other person's job easier.

You have also (by providing information that comes from your research) assume a position of "In Control."

That, my friends, is almost *magic!*

How many people do *you* know, in an interview situation, who know how to be *in control* in the salary situation?

►What Comes Next?

After you have provided this information, you *stop talking.*

Notice the interviewer's response, expression, and timing of his or her next words. Read the interviewer's eyes, as well as listen to the next words this person says.

If those next words are "That's no problem," you may have positioned yourself as "Too Low," "Too Inexpensive," or "Too Cheap."

Is it, now, too late? Are you "boxed in" to the range you have mentioned? No. Of course not.

You can negotiate fringe benefits, flexible time, additional vacation, profit sharing, bonuses, and virtually anything else.

You can even negotiate a much higher salary.

All you have said thus far is that:

"*Some people, in some organizations and in some situations, are earning money that generally ranges from X to Y, but that this amount may be considerably greater when everything else is figured in.*"

You have not stated that "I want _____" or that "I need _____ to live and to support my family."

Employers are not interested in your needs, your desire for a better home, your fulfilling a lifelong dream for a sports car, or in a list of your monthly expenses.

They are interested in solving their problems, in hiring the best possible person to do that, in hiring a person who "fits in," and in paying a reasonable amount of money to accomplish these things.

A word of warning: some employers are downright cheap. They were. They are. And they will continue to be. Watch out for them! They never change!

A young man I know works for one of them. He's always the #1 or #2 producer in sales. His performance is excellent, and so is his knowledge of his field. But he makes under $20,000 annually, and he's afraid to change employers.

He has a college degree in psychology and is attractive and intelligent, but he works for an employer who has been, is, and will be "cheap."

If you've done your homework correctly, you'll avoid wasting your time talking to people like this employer.

"New Age" employers realize that when their employees do well and are happy, employers and their organizations will do well and provide happy places in which to work.

"Old Age" employers build an organization by which and through which *they* can profit, and "the employees be damned."

Simple research and enlightening conversations with friends and associates can help you discover the "Old Age" employers before you solicit their fruitless favors and worthless workplaces.

►A Final Word on Money

The wiser you get, the more you realize that health and happiness are everything...and that money is nothing.

But at about the same time in your life, you will realize, or you may have already realized, that money is power...and that it often gives you the power to live a lifestyle that may create the possibility for you to have health and happiness.

You are not locked in.

You have the power of choice to do what you want, to do it where you want to do it, to do it by yourself, or to do it for an employer who, like you, recognizes the magnificence of life and supports and sustains the good things of life, which it can bring to anyone who makes these things a possibility for himself or herself.

Don't get the idea that your package is so important and is worth so much money that you never get the chance to get your package started. Ideas inflated with self-worth have ruined thousands of potential opportunities for job hunters.

But do have an honest recognition of the uniqueness of your potential.

And be willing to continue your journey toward that potential, either on your own, or within the universe of an employer, firm, or organization that allows you the joys of the journey.

Chapter 10
Electronic Job Banks

A Few Words on "The Latest Way to Job Hunt"

This chapter presents a slightly different *slant* on the new electronic job banks. In every period of time—be it a month, a season, a year, or a decade—billions of new ideas are created. Most of these are not very good and are forgotten almost as quickly as they came into being.

Some ideas last slightly longer and become fads. Hula hoops, magic pyramids ("put your dull razor blades under this hollow, palm-sized pyramid overnight, and they'll be sharp by morning!") bubble wands, Veg-A-Matic, the Pet Rock, Wall Walkers, home hair cutters, the Pocket Fisherman...you can probably name hundreds more.

In the 1990s, rapid improvements in electronic technology have given millions access to desktop computers, letter-quality (or even professional quality) printing, and software programs that do almost anything.

In the mid-1960s—the early days of solid state computers—a new concept was developed: a computer-based **"job bank."** Resumes and individual statistics and qualifications would become available to millions of prospective employers nationwide, even worldwide.

It began to look as though the horrible task of job hunting would be (thankfully!) finished forever. Job banks gave us hope that we might be able to avoid the overwhelming task of writing and sending out hundreds of resumes. Or, even more importantly, that we might avoid all those depressing rejections usually received from companies and organizations to which we applied.

In a job bank, someone would list your resume free or for a small fee; employers would then access, examine, and screen qualify candidates instantly, electronically. Employers would, theoretically, *come to you,* eliminating the dreaded pavement pounding, the typing or copying of countless resumes, and the writing and typing of each cover letter. Voila! Job banks would get rid of *all those things we **hated** to do.*

"Wow! This is gonna be **GREAT!**"

But: ooooooops!

Here it is, now, thirty years later.

Yes, there **are** centrally filed electronic resume systems.

Yes, job banks do exist.

We now have something even better: electronic facsimile machines (nicknamed fax) to send paperwork and correspondence all over the world—resumes and cover letters included—instantly.

Don't be surprised when you're asked to fax your resume, but that means you lose the advantage of doing it on wonderful paper—the touch, the feel, and the impression we've hammered into you for these pages thus far.

Go ahead: fax it, and then follow up with the "real thing" immediately, sent through the mail, by overnight express, or whatever method seems appropriate, "for your files." Take advantage of the opportunity you have in sending the real resume to thank readers for their time, using an enclosed card and envelope, a Post-It note, or some other means of saying thank-you.

But what happened to the notion that electronics and centralized job banks would "take over?" That the drudgery of looking and looking and looking…applying, applying, applying…and being rejected, and rejected, and rejected, would be eliminated? What about the idea that employers would come to you, instead of your having to go to them (and beg!)? What *happened* to this brilliant utopian idea?

It didn't work. It probably never will. Not even in these days of on-line, Internet, and fax machines in gas stations.

Employers seemed to like the idea of instant access to thousands of resumes, as much as you and I. In theory, it would save them time and money.

But in practice, employers have always preferred, just as you would if you were hiring someone, to know more about the *person* behind the resume.

Electronic job banks have been created, have grown, and now account for far more activity than in their beginning. Possibly, they may even be responsible for a significant increase in the amount of actual job placements.

But are **you** better off using them than not using them? The odds remain about the same for job hunters using electronic job systems and job banks as the odds when they are using other methods for obtaining employment. Those odds are **terrible.**

Many candidates' resumes (hundreds, thousands, tens of thousands, maybe millions) are reviewed, many screened, few make the cut, and *only one* is hired. That person hired may, *or may not,* be from "the electronic pool."

Does this sound like the perfect job hunting system to you? It doesn't and it isn't. It's the same old thing: hundreds apply, few make the cut, and one is chosen.

If you use an electronic job bank, do employers actually "come to you?" No. Not many. Some? Yes. But very few do or will.

If you are highly qualified in a specific field, especially a field where it is difficult to find people to hire, or if you are extremely well educated and hold a degree from a prestigious university, your credentials may stand out, and you may make the "electronic cut." (That is, your resume may be selected because you used the right words, just as the I.R.S. may select your tax return to audit because you used certain words they find to be indicative of people who tend to owe more tax than they remit).

The words used to select candidates are entirely at the discretion of the employer; the words may be "solenoid," "artificial intelligence," "20 years experience," "chemical engineering," or "dairy products." Or they may even be "play racquetball," "Harvard University," or "Notre Dame football." These latter words are unlikely, of course, but possible.

The basic tenet remains that the electronic job hunting systems are one, and *only* one, of many possible options. They didn't exist fifty years ago, so they **are** new and far more sophisticated, and perhaps more effective *now* than they were twenty years ago. But they are probably no more effective than any other system of job hunting.

They do give you exposure, and they do save you the task of writing cover letters, and they may save you from spending some postage or overnight express money. But the results are likely to be poor.

Summary: Relatively few people will *ever* obtain employment through the electronic systems because **"many** are screened, **few** are selected, and **one** is hired."** There, we've said it enough.

On-line services—for example, CompuServe, America Online, Prodigy, Internet, or any of the thousands of private bulletin boards—are also potential sources of employment. For a comprehensive and valuable overview of the changes that electronics is making in job search techniques, see *Electronic Job Search Revolution,* which is one of two new books by syndicated columnist Joyce Lain Kennedy and her colleague Thomas J. Morrow. Joyce is the acknowledged journalist-of-choice regarding the job market, and she and Morrow have captured the essence of the latest technologies being used in hiring and job hunting. These technologies and their applications include electronic resume databases; software systems used to track applicants within (usually large) employers; on-line job banks and classified "help wanted" advertising; electronic career centers; and even electronic interviews.

Use these new technologies, indeed. But beware. A basic rule of effective job hunting is that you must take charge of your own job hunt, just as you must take charge of your own life—as Richard Bolles points out in *What Color Is Your Parachute?* Popping your resume into an electronic hopper requires minimal effort and usually yields minimal results! In this method, you turn over your job hunt to another person or a machine. When someone else does the work, or is supposed to, the result usually yields little benefit for you.

Finally, the electronic job hunting system may actually prevent you from using some of your most valuable tools.

1. You aren't using your **personal contact network.** Networking—that is, "who you know"—accounts for more than 80 percent of all new

hires. Why place faith in a method that produces jobs for only a small fraction of the other 20 percent?

2. When you use an electronic system, you probably don't show yourself off in the best possible light. We recommend that you use superior quality paper for your resume, and that you choose your color/weight/consistency of paper very carefully. We recommend that you use an easily readable typeface in tandem with this top-quality paper. We recommend that you use an attractive stamp. In short, we think you should have a 100-percent perfect "package" representing you. An electronic readout, or a curled-up fax sheet, or a poorly reproduced copy from a computer printer, does little to lend excellence to your packaging.

3. Your resume may, if it's selected at all, be selected by an employer whose reputation for quality, or for treating employees well, or for integrity, is below your standards. Using the electronic systems, "so that employers come to me, instead of my having to find them," does the very thing you should not be doing. It turns selecting over to *them* rather than where it belongs: with *you*.

Yes, we know that **you** will be making the ultimate decision to accept or decline a job offer, but take a moment, please, and learn this important fact of life:

THE CONTEXT IN WHICH YOU LEAD YOUR LIFE WILL DETERMINE THE OUTCOME OF YOUR LIFE,

OR

THE GAME YOU'RE PLAYING WILL DETERMINE HOW WELL YOU'LL DO.

Playing the game—any game—correctly is among the most important goals any of us should ever have. Your career is a game; life is a game; family and relationships, traveling, scheduling your week…are all games. Playing each according to its rules and knowing when to bend those rules will make or break most of us.

But playing the game isn't the **most** important thing. **Choosing** the game to play comes first.

If you choose the wrong game and play it well, you might still lose. Someone else may choose his or her game better and be more skilled at it than you. But if you choose the game well **and** play it perfectly, you're much more likely to win.

During my career, I've been fortunate enough to know "the right people" and had the opportunity to do some assignments in glamorous and elegant locales—jobs most people would covet. I escorted and led vacation tour groups and overseas trips while working for tour operators and travel agencies.

Inevitably, when I reveal this part of my background in my seminars, people come forward during the break, or after the program, to say, "Leading tours is my absolute dream job. It's what I've always wanted to do. How can I do it?"

After the program ends, I always offer to reveal the relatively easy steps to take to become a tour guide, but few ever go on to take them. Why? Because they'd like to be **given** the opportunity to do this kind of work. What I tell them involves taking several proactive steps—they must do the work them-selves—toward achieving this goal. They want free travel, but they don't want to do what it takes to get it. What foolishness!

From these seminar experiences, and from having traveled to other coun-tries more than forty times on my own, I can tell you that *there is a major difference between people who take an escorted or guided tour...and those who go independently.*

Not only is there a big difference between the escorted and independent travelers, *there is a major difference in the ATTITUDE of a person on a tour. An attitude very different from that of* **the very same person** *who, the follow-ing year, travels independently.*

People on a tour expect that things will be done **for** them: their luggage will be handled, their rooms will be waiting, meals will be served, and sight-seeing will be arranged. (By the way, this *is* a pleasant way to travel, if you can afford it.)

The independent traveler, however, knows that *he* or *she* is responsible for the success of the trip. The person on a tour feels that the tour leader is responsible for the trip's success—and for the traveler's own happiness.

So what does all of this mean to you?

The analogy is this: If you turn over your job hunt to a computer, an employment agency, a job bank, or to anything or anyone other than yourself, your context becomes the view that "I'm not responsible for the ultimate suc-cess of this undertaking."

So, you'll probably slack off a bit when it comes to doing the nitty-gritty work that successful job hunters almost always do: thorough investigations of employers. Employers who, through the agency or job bank or any other third-party method, interview you or even offer you employment.

If you take this easier route, the context of the game you are playing and the way you choose to play become **nonresponsibility.** Therefore, you are probably engaging in *less effective and less-than-totally-responsible* behav-iors, which will almost always yield **less-than-optimum results.**

There you have it. The latest and most electronically sophisticated meth-ods of job hunting appear extremely tempting. They look easy and especially appealing because they mean "a lot less work." So, do I recommend that you avoid them completely?

Not exactly.

I merely recommend not placing much faith in these techniques. I think it is **unlikely** that they will lead you to the best job you've ever had or to the best employer in the state.

Just because they're new, or cheap, or easy, or a shortcut, or "the latest," doesn't make them the best.

Try every method you can. But put your greatest efforts behind the ones that will most likely yield the best results.

▶The Primary Advantage of Electronic Resumes and Job Banks

Electronic resumes, and resumes scanned electronically, do have a major advantage: SPEED.

When you put your resume into the job bank, employers can call up and quickly scan thousands of resumes in the time it might take someone to read ten or twenty of the "regular" kind.

So it's quite possible that this method will become somewhat popular, if only because it will save employers time and, therefore, money.

The style in which you write for the electronic scanner, however, is considerably different from the style you would use for a "regular" resume.

The book to read to learn everything about this specialized style is *Electronic Resume Revolution,* a second book by Joyce Lain Kennedy and Thomas J. Morrow. This book tells you, more completely than any other source, about the important **keywords** concept.

It's this: The electronic scanner goes through your resume lightning fast, looking for only certain **keywords.** It may even be looking for several instances of the same word.

It might be looking for such keywords as these:

> Mechanical engineer
> Biomedical technician
> Shrinkwrap packaging engineer
> Sales manager, foreign cars
> Mercedes-Benz
> The Kellogg School of Business
> Northwestern University
> Harvard University Medical School
> Deloitte & Touche
> Arthur Andersen
> Andersen Consulting
> McKinsey & Company
> International food marketing and distribution
> Procter & Gamble
> ISO 9000
> Quality Circles

If a company wanted a person who had worked for Proctor & Gamble (P&G "alumni" are considered by many to be extremely well trained in consumer products marketing, so it might not be unusual for someone heading a smaller company to want to hire such a person), the computer could screen thousands of resumes very quickly, selecting only those that contain the Proctor & Gamble name.

Therefore, the resume writer who uses a job bank or on-line method *must* be aware of the "looking for the right words and eliminating everyone else" factor. The resume must be written with *very specific, highly recognizable,* and *highly marketable* words that the applicant knows are **in demand.**

It may even be that the person writing a resume for scanners should *repeat* phrases, names, institutions, or computer systems known to be in demand. Scanning machines may be programmed to select only resumes that mention a particular factor, name, technique, or company more than once. Think about what the employers might be looking for, and create your resume to give it to them.

►What Electronic Resumes Look Like

An electronic resume looks like a regular resume, except that an electronic resume should include certain keywords: words that the computer or scanning device will "see." You should use those words several times in your resume, so it's more likely that they will be "seen."

If you have worked in several computer systems or know several software programs, mention them at least once and probably more than once.

The section on keywords alone in Joyce Lain Kennedy and Thomas J. Morrow's book, *Electronic Resume Revolution,* is probably worth the price of the book. On page after page, keywords are listed under subject headings. You won't find every word or subject, but you'll see more on a topic that takes greater space and time than I have in this book.

You should know what an electronically targeted resume looks like, though, and how it "reads" differently than regular resumes. On the next few pages are samples to inspect. The resumes' keywords—the words the scanning device or computer will be seeking—are listed in **boldface type.** It should be noted, though, that some scanning devices do not easily pick up boldface type; therefore, I do not recommend using it. Note, too, that the sample resumes are not real resumes; they were created only as examples of scannable types.

Sarah Rollins Wells
1447 Columbine Way
Charleston, South Carolina
(000) 555-7890

Career Objective: Purchasing Manager

May, 19xx
to
Present

Purchasing Manager
Rambo Military Uniform Company
Desert Storm, South Carolina

- **Purchased** cloth fabric and other materials for **$100-million-sales** military contract manufacturer: cotton, wool, synthetics, plus special military products to specifications.

- Interviewed, recommended, and selected all **vendors and suppliers**; dealt with 9 primary and 17 secondary vendors.

- Reduced costs 9% first year, **cost reductions of 11.5%** second year; **saved $672,000/year**; implemented new **cost-control** systems; received "Outstanding Employee Award" (given for efficiency-improvement/cost savings).

June, 19xx
to
May, 19xx

Assistant Purchasing Manager
Arlington Fabric Factory
Wrong Turn, North Carolina

- Responsible for **purchasing** for four regional areas (1/3 of total regions) of national **men's, women's, and children's clothing retailer.**

- **Saved $120,000** by developing new computerized buying/purchasing system for vendor selection and tracking.

- **Wrote Purchasing Manual** now in use (64 pages) for all divisions of the corporation. Received commendation of superiors for "your outstanding work, writing the finest purchasing manual of its kind we have seen."

Scott J. Kenneth
783 North Forest Trail
Quinto Ridge, California 98764
(000) 555-3456

<u>Job Objective: Creative Director, Advertising Agency</u>

May, 19xx
to
Present

<u>Creative Director</u>
Wallow, Inne, Mudd Creative Group
Los Angeles, California

- Complete responsibility for all creative work in **$15-million** (annual billings) **advertising agency** specializing in **consumer accounts**.

- Produce **TV commercials** for **local, regional, and national** accounts: **10-15-30-60 second spots**.

- Winner, Los Angeles Advertising Club, **"Creative Director of the Year"** Award.

- Winner, two **CLIO Awards** for TV commercials.

- **Supervise 3 copywriters**; set strategy for 22 clients; write and edit ad copy, scripts.

- Select **photographers, illustrators, TV production teams**, all other outside contractors for all clients.

- **Interview, hire, and train** all creative personnel, traffic coordinators, etc.

- Meet with clients, prospective clients; create, produce, and present all presentations for prospective agency clients.

- Personally responsible for "closing" **8 new clients** in six years with the agency. Considered primarily responsible for agency's growth from **$5 million to $15 million** annual billings during this period.

April, 19xx
to
April, 19xx

<u>Assistant Creative Director</u>
Summ, Lotta, Nerv Advertising Agency
Compton, California

References are available from business, educational, personal, and creative sources and will be gladly furnished on request. "Creative Book and Reel" available.

▶How Important Are the New Electronic Techniques?

We are only beginning to use and implement these new techniques and changes, but my personal prediction is that nothing, ever, will take the place of personal contacts and "knowing the job, knowing the employer, knowing the field, and knowing the individuals who have the power to hire."

We've said, for years, that you should "never allow any piece of paper, no matter how good a resume or cover letter may be, to take the place of, or to come between, you and the employer, face-to-face." That's still true.

It's much easier to say "no" by mail, or even over the phone, than it is to reject a candidate in person—especially if that person is a personal acquaintance or friend.

That's why electronics may not be the technique-of-choice for you. It is, however, an increasingly important part of job-search, and that's why we recommend that you take a few moments to become familiar with it by reading the two books by Kennedy and Morrow.

Is it necessary for you to read this material, and know about this right now? Probably not. Would I buy or read the book anyway? Yes, absolutely. You cannot afford to *not* know about these methods, and you cannot afford to not know how to write your resume so that the scanner will select you "in" rather than reject you "out."

Chapter 11
The New Job Market for the Last Half of the '90s

What to Expect in the 21st Century

Want to predict the future? We've been reasonably accurate in our guesses and predictions about the job market since first holding workshops and speaking engagements in 1975. Even though this is a resume book, you might want to pay attention to this brief chapter concerning trends in future years, and what to expect in the 21st century.

- The **rate of change,** the speed at which new ideas, systems, inventions, technologies, and discoveries appear and either soon disappear, or become a part of our fast-moving civilization, will increase dramatically!

- **Television** will progress far beyond local channels or cable on a box in a room. You'll gain access to virtually anywhere. TV will offer *instant access* to hundreds of programs, educational courses, movies, and more. There will be no more waiting for 7:00 p.m. on Wednesday for your favorite program.

- **TV** will be wall-sized if you desire. It will zoom in and out to whatever you want to see.

- With your **computer,** you'll use TV to watch, say, a travelog on Sweden. You'll then be able to request additional information on any subject: highways, restaurants, conversion rates, history, etc. You'll be able to call up instant information, movies, and interactive Q&A

possibilities. Obviously, computers will be faster, lighter, better...almost all-powerful. **You won't be able to compete without them!**

- **Telephones** will become so futuristic and versatile that today's phones will look like Fisher-Price toys. The forthcoming combinations of telephones, pagers, computers, laser printers, and TVs will revolutionize virtually everything we do and know.

- **Downsizing** will continue into the foreseeable future. There's no end in sight for growing "leaner and meaner."

- **Medium-sized and smaller-sized companies** will be the next wave of companies forced to cut back on labor costs, fringe benefits, and other expenses.

- **Competition will grow** more intense in virtually every field. Everyone will have to market herself or himself! If you don't know how to market, start learning about it *now.*

- **Good companies will become smaller** with each passing year, not larger as the trend has been during the 20th century. In the 1950s, cars and companies grew bigger each year and were perceived as "better than before." In the future, smaller firms will continue to proliferate.

- **Jobs will decrease in number** because the majority of jobs exist in large companies—that's the bad news. The good news is that there will be ***more work that needs to be done.*** So, there will be no lack of opportunity for work or to earn a living. Yet it will be harder to find the places that pay to get things done. To find work in the 1950s, all you did was "go downtown." Now, downtown has exploded into a metropolitan area, and large companies have disbanded into thousands of smaller ones.

- **More people will work temporary jobs,** or be "available on contract." Job security will become less attainable; therefore, you'll have more excitement in your life. That's both good and bad: being on a roller coaster is fun for five minutes, but it might not be so great year after year.

- **The education system will change dramatically;** there will be a revolution in the ways people learn. School systems and educational costs have become prohibitive, and we will find alternative ways—better ways—to accomplish learning objectives.

▶What's Needed to Get Ahead

If you want to know what's needed to get ahead **in these complicated years,** here are some tips:

- **Education.** Finish school, enroll in a college or university, graduate, and earn an advanced degree too if you can. Take courses and major in things you like, not in "a field that pays a lot."

- **Constant learning *after* you graduate.** Continue to read books, professional magazines, and business-related material; attend seminars and training events; and take courses. The more you learn, the better protected you will be in even more competitive times. Don't expect the company to provide training; **you** will probably be responsible for the improvement of your product. This is relatively new. Companies in the 1950s expected to keep you for 40 years; today they know it's likely that you'll leave, or they'll have to let you go. Therefore, the training they probably *should* be doing may be left up to you.

- **Possess great communication skills**—not just good ones but great ones. Know your English and be able to write clearly with correct grammar and spelling. Learn to speak in front of others and to make points with clarity, conciseness, and good humor. Great communicators get ahead much faster than those who lie in the weeds waiting to be discovered.

- **Be computer smart.** If you're not, you'll be left behind—way behind!

- **Network!** Join groups, organizations, and civic clubs. Be active in them, not passive. Volunteer for committees, charities, etc. When things get tough, your company lays off, or your own business runs into trouble, you'll have a powerful support group of people who may know where you can find work.

- **Keep your record clean.** Watch your behaviors and actions, and recognize things you may be doing that you wouldn't want to be questioned about. Recognize any errant ways and change them. NOW.

- **Thank people** along the way; be appreciative of others and generous to those who have less than you. You will need friends during your life, and these are small prices to pay for that privilege. Write at least one thank-you note each week, and stay in touch with "networking friends."

- **Be global in your thinking.** Travel internationally, even if it requires sacrifices. The first time you get off a plane overseas, you will be amazed...at virtually everything.

- **Understand that marketing rules the roost.** "Nothing happens until someone sells something" is an old proverb and a wise statement. Know your products, know your markets, and understand that *people buy* **benefits** *rather than products and services.*

- **Productive people are the first hired and the last to go.** How do you become more productive? Do what you enjoy doing!

- **Quality counts.** If someone else's quality record is better than yours, you won't get ahead, and he or she will. Achieving quality the first time is a lot easier than doing a slipshod job and repairing it later.

- **Model yourself after people you admire—people with values.** It's easy to admire lightweights, but people of substance are the ones you should emulate. Choose your heroes carefully. Your subconscious guides you to be like them even when you're not aware of it.

That's it. Thanks for being with us, we appreciate the time you've spent here. Now, go live your life the right way, and don't let anyone stand in your way or tell you that you can "get away with it."

The ultimate lesson in life is that you can't get away with **anything.** Leading a good life, helping or serving others, is the sure way to getting where you want to go—now and hereafter.

Dave Swanson

Epilogue
Is This the End?

This is the final chapter.

But this isn't the end.

Having a Purpose

People who know, people far more knowledgeable than I am, tell us that life is more worth while, more satisfying, and more productive if it has a *purpose*.

A purpose means that you have a *vision* of where you hope to go in your life...what you hope to *be* and *become*.

In the 1970s a certain brewery told us that "You only go around once in life, so grab for all the *gusto* you can!"

If they meant *aliveness,* I think they were right on target.

Life is about being *alive* and about living your *purpose*.

Job hunting, too, should have a *purpose*.

A specific goal.

Adopting "A Philosophy of Job Hunting"

And it is best lived out if you adopt a Philosophy of Job Hunting, a kind of *purpose* for doing what you are going to do.

May I suggest a philosophy for your job hunt?

"What must I do to make certain that I am the number one candidate for this job?"

So if you are in doubt about whether to do that little extra something that would make you #1, now you know what to do.

Do it!

And do it right!

You have a **duty** to yourself to do your best!

Millions of advertising dollars have been spent to impress people with two philosophies that apply more to life than they do to hamburgers.

"You deserve a break today."

"You! You're the One!"

And you are! You are the one who can give yourself the break you deserve.

Most folks take every little bump in the road as a signal to turn back and go home.

So they spend much of their life going back where they started.

Circumstances don't make lives good. Or bad.

It's what you do with the circumstances that makes a difference.

▶Empowering Yourself

In my seminars, some people actually complain that we talk about *empowerment* and about "doing something *special* with your life" rather than just existing in it.

Peter Ueberroth, winner of *TIME's* "Man of the Year" award and the man who turned the Olympics in Los Angeles into a phenomenal success, gives us a valuable lesson when he says:

"Authority is only 20 percent given, and it is 80 percent taken!"

Don't wait for someone to give you something.

Take responsibility for taking it.

Take it honestly.

Earn it.

Do it with integrity.

Life isn't easy.

But it *is* always an adventure if you choose to make it one.

▶Acting

Psychologist and positive thinker Denis Waitley talks of the "poor TV watcher," sitting there, bored to tears, and wasting a life, wasting so many talents.

While actors and actresses in a far-away studio have the time of their lives. Being well-paid.

And doing what they love most—acting.

Act!

Living is an *active* art!

The more you *do* in this life, the happier and more satisfied you will be.

The more you give to others, the happier *you* will be.

And the more you devote your activities to the things you love to do *most* and do *best,* the fuller and more productive your life will become.

And you will contribute to the goodwill being done on the planet.

▶Living

Existence is the booby prize.

Living is First Place!

If you don't *live,* you lose.

Be a winner.

Then you'll never worry about having to say, "I can't remember what I wanted to be when I grew up…, but I know this isn't it."

Take charge of your life.

Make it living **Alive.**

Make it work for you!

Appendix
Dave Swanson's QUICK GUIDE to Using Resumes

1. Don't EVER allow a resume to come *between* you and a job…or between you and a potential employer. NO piece of paper can, or should, take the place of a personal contact. Resumes should (1) make a superior impression; and (2) get you inside so that the employer can *see* what you look like, how you present yourself, how you speak, how focused your career goals are, what you're like, etc. *If you can discover a way to do these (that is, get in to see the person),* **without using a resume first,** *by all means DO IT!*

2. If you do send a resume, include a cover letter. The cover letter should either compensate for things not mentioned (or only partially explained) or highlight the most important items from your resume that are *relevant to this job.*

3. Your resume should be printed on *superior* quality paper. Your cover letter should be typed on a *superior* quality typewriter or an A+++ letter-quality or laser printer. Anything less will not do. The screener is looking for ways to keep you out—not to help get you in—and may resort to *any* reason for doing so.

4. Your cover letter should be typed or laser printed on paper of similar high quality. Nothing less will do.

5. Your cover letter should be no more than one-third of a page in length. It must be perfect like your resume. To eliminate any spelling mistakes, have someone proofread both your resume and your cover letter. Don't take chances! One mistake could possibly cost you a $50,000 job.

6. If you're *tempted* to send a resume to a situation where you don't know the name of the employer, you're not following Rule #1: NETWORK! Learn the name of someone in the department you want to work in, and network your way into his or her office. Before you do, know as much as possible about the organization, the field it is in, the new trends in that field, the competitors, and the organization's problems. Be prepared!

7. If you are sending a resume to a blind P.O. box, or if you are in a situation where you do not know the name of the employer to whom you are writing:

   a. You will probably NOT receive a reply. Also, be certain that you're not sending your resume to the place where you currently work!

   b. Your resume will probably not be read for a while, perhaps as many as 10 to 20 days *after* the ad ran.

   c. If hundreds (or thousands) of replies are received (as is *normal*), your resume may not be read at all. Someone, before he or she gets down to yours in the stack of resumes received, may conclude that "we've read enough."

   d. If you do receive a reply, it will probably take several weeks. If potential employers are in a *big rush*, they'll probably call you, so have your household prepared to answer the phone professionally and in a businesslike manner. Speak clearly—nothing funny, nothing vulgar—and have the TV and radio turned off before the phone is answered. If you use an answering machine, record a professional message and make certain the machine is working properly!

   e. You are almost always 100 percent out of control in a job search if you reply to any blind box number and do not know the organization to which you are responding (the blind box gives employers 100 percent control).

   f. You should probably reply *immediately* after you see the ad and then *again* in 10 days or so, with the exact *same resume and a clearly marked "COPY"* of your cover letter, topped with a Post-It note or a memo. This should say something like "Here's a copy of my resume and letter from two weeks ago, in case you missed my first response. I'm very interested in this job and look forward to hearing from you soon. Thank you."

8. Weird resumes are presumed, in most cases, to be written by weird people.

9. Classy resumes are presumed to be written by classy people.

10. Many professional resume writers are less competent than you might expect. Go to several and compare. Watch out before you spend your hard-earned money on an inferior product produced by people who know little more about this than you do—or, in some cases, less. We know an applicant who had his resume redone by six different (professional?) writers over a two-year period. None of the six resumes was very good, and prices ranged from $75 to $375. The problem was "the person," not "the resume." (He, of course, blamed the resume.)

Using the Internet in Your Job Search

by Fred E. Jandt and Mary Nemnich

This is the definitive, hands-on guide for job seekers with access to the Internet. *Using the Internet in Your Job Search* explains how to:

- Connect to the Internet
- Find job listings and research potential employers on the Internet
- Use news groups to get leads
- Adapt standard resumes to an electronic format and capture reader attention in the first screen

This guide book also contains valuable advice on how to use e-mail to contact potential employers and make a good impression; legal and ethical issues of the e-mail job search; and the psychology of using the Internet in a job search.

Other Information

- One in every three U.S. households has a personal computer.
- CompuServe, Prodigy, and America Online have 11 million users.
- Millions of other people have noncommercial access to the Internet.

> 7 1/2 x 9 1/2, Paper, 240 pp.
> **ISBN 1-56370-173-1**
> **$16.95** Order Code J1731

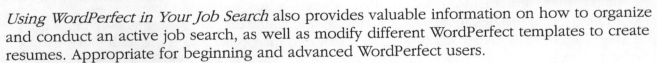

Using WordPerfect in Your Job Search

by David F. Noble

This is a new, focused kind of computer book that shows readers how to use the power of WordPerfect to create best-quality resumes, cover letters, and other important job search documents. Detailed, step-by-step instructions make it easy to create many different types of resumes, such as:

- Chronological resumes
- Combination resumes
- Resumes from templates
- Scannable resumes
- Hypertext resumes

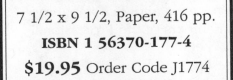

Using WordPerfect in Your Job Search also provides valuable information on how to organize and conduct an active job search, as well as modify different WordPerfect templates to create resumes. Appropriate for beginning and advanced WordPerfect users.

> 7 1/2 x 9 1/2, Paper, 416 pp.
> **ISBN 1 56370-177-4**
> **$19.95** Order Code J1774

Other Information

- Step-by-step instructions on how to use WordPerfect to create and desktop publish quality resumes and other job search documents
- Contains many examples of resumes, cover letters, and other job search documents

Look for these and other fine books from JIST Works, Inc., at your full service bookstore or call us for additional information at 800-648-5478.

The Quick Interview & Salary Negotiation Book
Dramatically Improve Your Interviewing Skills and Pay in a Matter of Hours
by J. Michael Farr

More than 80 percent of job applicants do a poor job of presenting their skills in job interviews. Even more people are baffled by problem questions, such as:

- What salary are you expecting?
- Why should I hire you?
- What is your major weakness?

The simple yet powerful three-step process explained in this book unravels the secret of answering these and other difficult interview questions. *The Quick Interview & Salary Negotiation Book* contains features that will enable readers to quickly improve their interviewing skills and avoid being screened out of a job before the interview.

Other Information
- Includes basic and advanced interview techniques
- Contains many specific examples
- Helps develop a powerful skills language

> 7 x 9, Paper, 220 pp.
> **ISBN 1-56370-162-6**
> **$9.95** Order Code J1626

• •

Gallery of Best Resumes
A Collection of Quality Resumes by Professional Resume Writers
by David F. Noble

A showcase collection of quality resumes for those seeking a job or changing careers. *Gallery of Best Resumes* contains outstanding examples of different types of resumes for a variety of occupations grouped by category, such as Accounting/Finance, Administrative Assistant/Secretary, Graduating/Graduated Student, Management, etc. Includes helpful tips and techniques consistently used in the best resumes. A set of sample resumes printed on high-quality paper stock is bound right into the book.

> 8 1/2 x 11, Paper 416 pp.
> **ISBN 1-56370-144-8**
> **$16.95** Order Code GBR

Other Information
- Contains more than 200 resumes and 25 companion cover letters written by members of the Professional Association of Resume Writers
- Features 101 best resume tips
- Highlights 30 tips for polishing cover letters

Look for these and other fine books from JIST Works, Inc., at your full service bookstore or call us for additional information at 800-648-5478.